Real Peace

Other titles by Warren W. Wiersbe

Real Peace

Freedom and Conscience in the Christian Life

Warren W. Wiersbe

Baker Books

A Division of Baker Book House Co
Grand Rapids, Michigan 49516

© 2003 by Warren W. Wiersbe

Published by Baker Books
A division of Baker Book House Company
P.O. Box 6287, Grand Rapids, MI 49516-6287
www.bakerbooks.com

Printed in the United States of America

Library of Congress Cataloging-in-Publication Data
Wiersbe, Warren W.
    Real peace : freedom and conscience in the Christian life / Warren W. Wiersbe.
        p.   cm.
    ISBN 0-8010-6438-4 (pbk.)
    1. Christian life. 2. Liberty—Religious aspects—Christianity. 3. Conscience—Religious aspects—Christianity. I. Title.
BV4501.3 .W542 2002
241′.1—dc21   2002013151

Unless otherwise indicated, Scripture is taken from the *New Scofield Reference Bible.*

Scripture marked nasb is taken form the NEW AMERICAN STANDARD BIBLE ®. Copyright © The Lockman Foundation 1960, 1962, 1963, 1968, 1971, 1972, 1973, 1975, 1977, 1995. Used by permission.

Contents

Preface

This book contains edited transcriptions of radio messages I delivered over the Back to the Bible international network.

These messages were first spoken to a listening audience make up of a variety of people in many nations and at many stages of spiritual growth. This explains the brevity, simplicity, and directness of the material. Were I writing a comementary or presenting a longer pulpit message, the approach would be vastly different.

In sending out these messages, my prayer is that they will encourage and build up God's people and help them in their own ministries.

Part 1

Freedom

1

What Is Freedom?

While window-shopping one day, I saw a T-shirt with beautiful butterflies printed on it. The lettering on the T-shirt read: "Butterflies are free!" Of course, butterflies are free! *They are free to be butterflies,* but they certainly aren't free to fly to the moon!

Our world is concerned about freedom, but very few people ask, "What really is freedom?" or, "If I did have freedom, how would I use it?" Here is what the Lord Jesus Christ had to say about freedom:

As he spoke these words, many believed on him. Then said Jesus to those Jews who believed on him, If ye continue in my word, then are ye my disciples indeed; and ye shall know the truth, and the truth shall make you free. They answered him, We are Abraham's seed, and were never in bondage to any man. How sayest thou, ye shall be made free? Jesus answered them, Verily, verily, I say unto you,

Whosoever committeth sin is the servant of sin. And the servant abideth not in the house forever; but the Son abideth ever. If the son, therefore, shall make you free, ye shall be free indeed.

John 8:30–36

The people to whom Jesus was speaking were confused about freedom. Imagine a Jewish person saying, "We have never been in bondage to any man!" When you read the Old Testament history, you find that the Jewish nation was often in bondage because God had to discipline them. In fact, at the very hour our Lord was speaking, the Jewish nation was under the heel of the Roman government!

Many people do not understand freedom. If you want to understand and enjoy freedom, you must understand the three affirmations that the Lord Jesus Christ made in this passage of Scripture: (1) God's purpose for people is freedom; (2) God's method for freedom is truth; and (3) God's revelation of truth is Jesus Christ.

God's Purpose for People

God's purpose for people is freedom. What is freedom? Many people think that freedom is the absence of restraint, but that could lead to anarchy. Suppose we had no laws telling us on what side of the highway to drive. Suppose we had no regulations governing such things as medicine or money. Suppose we were able to do whatever we wanted to do. The world would be filled with chaos! Freedom is not the absence of restraint, nor is freedom doing whatever you please. That could be the greatest kind of selfish bondage. *Freedom is the privilege and power to become all that God wants you to become. Freedom is the opportunity to fulfill your potential to the glory of God.*

12

You were born with a tremendous potential. When you were born again through faith in Jesus Christ, God added spiritual gifts to your natural talents. God surrounds you with opportunity. You and I are free in Jesus Christ, not to do whatever we want but to be all that God wants us to be. Freedom is the opportunity to fulfill your potential to the glory of God.

You were made in the image of God. God made you to be free. When God put the first man and woman in the garden, he gave them freedom—freedom that was governed by regulation, freedom that was hedged in by protective law. They were free to work for God. They were free to walk with God. But they were not free to disobey God so that they might have their own way. Creation says to me, "God made you to be free." We are made in the image of God to enjoy the freedom that he has made for us.

The Bible is a book of freedom. Beginning with the Exodus, when God set his people free, all the way through to the Book of Revelation, the emphasis is on freedom. Whenever the nation of Israel sinned, they found themselves in bondage. Whenever they obeyed God, they found themselves enjoying freedom. The Bible is a book of freedom. The cross speaks of freedom. The Holy City, the New Jerusalem, speaks of freedom. Every word in the New Testament pointing to Jesus Christ emphasizes freedom. Freedom begins with salvation, freedom begins with trusting Jesus Christ as your Savior.

Jesus said that whoever commits sin is the servant of sin (John 8:34). That verb means "is in the habit of practicing sin." In other words, when you and I repeatedly, continually disobey God, that isn't freedom; that's the worst kind of bondage. When you trust Jesus Christ as your Savior, you have freedom *from* the guilt, the punishment, the judgment of sin. You have freedom *in* walking with the Lord, in the Spirit, overcoming the power of sin. And you have freedom *to* become all that God wants you to become. You have freedom to grow, to develop your full potential and become like the Lord Jesus Christ. God's purpose for man is freedom.

God's Method for Freedom

God's method for freedom is truth. Two forces are at work in this world today—the force that comes from heaven and the force that comes from hell. The power of God works through truth, and the power of the Devil works through lies. Satan is the liar. Jesus made that very clear in John 8:44: "Ye are of your father the devil, and the lusts of your father ye will do. He was a murderer from the beginning, and abode not in the truth, because there is no truth in him. When he speaketh a lie, he speaketh of his own; for he is a liar, and the father of it."

Satan uses lies to bring you into bondage, and that bondage leads to destruction; but God uses truth to bring you into freedom, and that freedom leads to fulfillment. In Genesis 3 Satan said to our first parents, "Yea, hath God said?" (v. 1) and then he promised them, "Ye shall be as God" (v. 5). Satan was offering them freedom without responsibility, freedom without consequences, and there can be no such thing. Satan's lie is "Ye shall be as God," and that is the lie that rules the world today. Man is his own God. The world today is worshiping "the creature more than the Creator" (Rom. 1:25). Man no longer looks at himself as a creature who must be obedient to God. Man looks at himself as the creator. Man is now his own God! God's purpose for man is freedom, and God's method for freedom is truth.

Truth has been given to us in three different ways. In John 14:6 Jesus said, "I am . . . the truth." Jesus is the truth. This is why he claimed in John 8:36, "If the son,

14

therefore, shall make you free, ye shall be free indeed." This ties in with verse 32, "And ye shall know the truth, and the truth shall make you free." When you know Jesus Christ, you know God's living truth, and that truth sets you free.

The Word of God is truth. In John 17:17 our Lord said, "Sanctify them through thy truth; thy word is truth." This is why Jesus said in John 8:31–32, "If ye continue in my word, then are ye my disciples indeed; and ye shall know the truth, and the truth shall make you free." The Word of God is the truth of God. The Word of God also exposes the Devil's lies. When you and I have a personal relationship with the Son of God, we have truth. When we spend time studying and meditating on the Word of God, we discover the truth.

In 1 John 5:6, we are told that the Spirit is the truth. The Spirit of God gave us the Word of God. The Word of God is inspired by the Holy Spirit. The Holy Spirit of God teaches us the truth of the Word of God. "Where the Spirit of the Lord is, there is liberty" (2 Cor. 3:17). When the Spirit of God reveals the Son of God in the Word of God, we experience the freedom of God. God's method for freedom is truth. But let me warn you. Satan is at work with his lies, and Satan wants you to believe his lies. When you believe the truth and obey it, you experience freedom. When you believe the Devil's lies and obey them, then you experience bondage. God's purpose for man is freedom, and God's method for freedom is truth.

God's Revelation of Truth

Third, *God's revelation of truth is Jesus Christ.* "If the Son, therefore, shall make you free, ye shall be free indeed" (John 8:36). The Lord Jesus Christ could not make us free unless He were free Himself. When you read the four

[handwritten margin note:] The Holy Spirit takes the truth and drives it deep into our hearts so that it makes a difference.

Gospels, you see the experience of Jesus Christ here on earth, and He experienced freedom. He came to a nation that was under political bondage, but even more than that, it was under *spiritual* and *religious* bondage. The Pharisees had added so many traditions to the Word of God that the people were shackled. A yoke was put on the people that made it difficult for them to enjoy God. The Lord Jesus Christ was free from legalism. You don't see Him bowing down to the traditions of men. He was free from fear. He slept in a boat in the midst of a storm! He went to Calvary without fear. You don't see the Lord Jesus Christ in bondage to any person or system because He was free. "If the Son, therefore, shall make you free, ye shall be free indeed" (v. 36).

WRONG!!

The better you know the Lord Jesus Christ, the more freedom you are going to enjoy. Our responsibility is to know Him. How do you get to know Him? Through the Word of God. "Ye shall know the truth, and the truth shall make you free" (v. 32). Do you spend time daily in the Word of God? Are you studying the Word of God? Are you learning the Word of God? Have you discovered that the Word of God is your key to freedom? Get to *know* Him, and that word "know" doesn't simply mean to know intellectually. It means to have a living relationship with Him. Know Him. Trust Him. "If ye continue in my word, then are ye my disciples indeed" (v. 31). Yield to the Word of God. Try to do all that God wants you to do. It's important, very important, for the Word of God to fill our hearts and minds. We must know Him and we must trust Him.

We must love Him. "If God were your Father, ye would love me; for I proceeded forth and came from God; neither came I of myself, but he sent me" (v. 42). You see, the better we know Him, the more we trust Him. And the better we know Him, the more we love Him.

We should obey Christ. "If a man keep my saying, he shall never see death" (v. 51). That's an amazing statement, isn't it? Many Christians have died, but death was not an enemy. Death did not devour them or destroy them. Death was simply the open door that led to glory. Our responsibility is to know Jesus Christ better, to trust Him, to love Him, and to obey Him. When we have this living relationship with Jesus Christ, we begin to experience more and more of His freedom. This freedom we enjoy will be seen in our thinking, our speaking, our behaving. We experience joyful freedom, and we become more like the Lord Jesus Christ.

Now the interesting thing is this: the more you become like the Lord Jesus Christ, the more it releases your potential. We have yet to see what God can do in our lives! You may think you have no gifts or abilities. You may think there are no opportunities for you. You may be discouraged. But the more you become like Jesus Christ, the more you experience freedom. And the more freedom you experience, the more you release your own potential. Oh, the wonderful power and potential that God has put within you! *Freedom is life controlled by truth and motivated by love.* Bondage is life controlled by lies and motivated by selfishness. Freedom is the result of a living relationship with Jesus Christ—walking with Him, talking with Him, and learning from Him.

If you have never trusted Christ as your Savior, I would appeal to you to do so. Yield your life to Him. If you are already a Christian, you may be saying, "I don't want to be yielded to Christ. I want to live my own life." That's the worst kind of bondage. You see, sin's freedom is bondage, but bondage to Jesus Christ is true freedom. I want your life to be controlled by truth and motivated by love because, "If the Son, therefore, shall make you free, ye shall be free indeed" (v. 36).

2

False Freedom

Christian freedom is a life controlled by truth and motivated by love. It's the result of a growing relationship with Jesus Christ, who is the truth, and with the Word of God, and with the Holy Spirit of God, who is the Spirit of truth. But there is a false freedom in the world today, a freedom that comes not from heaven but from hell. Those who practice this false freedom have a life that is controlled by lies and motivated by lust.

This false freedom is described in 2 Peter 2.

But there were false prophets also among the people, even as there shall be false teachers among you, who secretly shall bring in destructive heresies, even denying the Lord that bought them, and bring upon themselves swift destruction. And many shall follow their pernicious ways, by reason of whom the way of truth shall be evil spoken of. And through covetousness shall they, with feigned words, make merchandise of you; whose judgment now for a long time lingereth not, and their destruction slumbereth not.

verses 1–3

These are wells without water, clouds that are carried with a tempest, to whom the mist of darkness is reserved forever. For when they speak great swelling words of vanity, they allure through the lusts of the flesh, through much wantonness, those that are just escaping from them who live in error. While they promise them liberty, they themselves are the servants of corruption; for of whom a man is overcome, of the same is he brought in bondage. For if, after they have escaped the pollutions of the world through the knowledge of the Lord and Savior, Jesus Christ, they are again entangled in it, and overcome, the latter end is worse with them than the beginning. For it had been better for them not to have known the way of righteousness than, after they have known it, to turn from the holy commandment delivered unto them. But it has happened unto them according to the true proverb, The dog is turned to his own vomit again; and the sow that was washed, to her wallowing in the mire.

verses 17–22

This is not a very beautiful picture is it? But it is one we need to look at because it contains a number of warnings we need to heed. These false teachers go after young Christians. Notice verse 18: "They allure through the lusts of the flesh, through much wantonness, those that are just escaping from them who live in error." They go after new believers and seek to lead them into a false freedom that turns into terrible bondage. Peter urged us to avoid this false freedom, and he gave three reasons why this freedom is dangerous.

19

Where False Freedom Comes From

False freedom is dangerous because of where it comes from. It comes from false teachers. Wherever you find the true, you find the false. Wherever you find the genuine, you will find the counterfeit. There were false prophets among the people of Israel, and there are going to be false teachers among Christians today. These teachers claim to believe in the Lord and follow the Word of God, and yet they so twist the Word of God and so misapply the Word of God that they lead people into bondage.

Notice what Peter said about these teachers, for he identified them accurately. In verse 1 these false teachers secretly introduce destructive heresies. They are not honest. They work in an underhanded way, and they deny the very Lord who died for them. This doesn't mean that these false teachers are saved. In fact, at the end of this chapter we find that they are not sheep; they are dogs and sows who have been washed, but they have never been changed into sheep. They are counterfeit. They are pretenders.

Verse 10 says that these people despise authority: "But chiefly them that walk after the flesh and the lust of uncleanness, and despise government. Presumptuous are they; self-willed, they are not afraid to speak evil of dignities." They are proud, boastful people who think they are the only ones who are right. They deny the Lord and despise authority, and they defile everything they touch. They walk in the lust of uncleanness, according to 2 Peter 2:10. Throughout 2 Peter 2 this description is given of uncleanness, perniciousness, wickedness, and evil. Of course, the worst part is that they are deceived and that they are deceivers. They deceive others because they are deceived themselves! It's a tragic picture.

According to verse 3, they use "feigned words." The Greek word translated "feigned" *(plastos)* is the word from which we get the English word "plastic." What are plastic words? They are words that can be twisted around to mean anything. The false teachers use our vocabulary but not our dictionary. When they talk about freedom or salvation or sin, they are not defining those words the way we do. They have plastic words.

"They . . . make merchandise of you," says verse 3. They're just out to make money! In fact, verses 14 and 18 tell me that they entice people. They beguile and allure unstable souls. They "speak great swelling words of vanity." These people promote their lies to make merchandise of young Christians and lead them astray. In verse 17 he compared them to wells without water and to clouds that promise rain but don't give any. Verse 13 says, "They are spots in your love feasts," blemishes in the body of the believers. They pretend to be Christians, but all they want to do is use religion as a means of making money and leading people into sin.

Beware of this false freedom because of where it comes from. It comes from false teachers who despise the authority of the Word of God, who will defile you, who will deceive you. They will lead you into depravity. They will entice you and allure you with their plastic words, their arrogant words, their empty words. They are religious racketeers.

What False Freedom Offers

Beware of this false freedom, not only because of where it comes from *but also because of what it offers.*

Freedom without Responsibility

What are they offering to people? They are offering them *freedom without responsibility,* and that's a dangerous thing. Whatever gives you freedom without adding to your self-control will lead you into bondage and destruction. The Prodigal Son wanted freedom, but he didn't want responsibility. There can be no true freedom without responsibility. Unearned freedom is a dangerous, destructive thing. This is what Satan offered our first parents in the Garden of Eden—freedom without responsibility. "Why would you listen to God? Has God said that you shall not eat of this tree? Exercise your freedom. You can get away with it!" (see Gen. 3:1, 4–5). Beware of anyone who offers you freedom without responsibility.

Freedom without Reckoning

They also offer *freedom without reckoning.* They say there will not be any judgment. "You're not going to face God and have to answer for this!" Sometimes they even use the Bible to teach their pernicious false doctrines. They say something like this: "After all, we live by grace, don't we? We're saved by grace, and we're not under Law. Therefore, we can live any way we please." Paul answered that in Romans 6:1–2: "What shall we say then? Shall we continue in sin, that grace may abound? God forbid."

Freedom without Repercussions

False grace leads to false freedom, and this freedom will have a day of reckoning. So they're offering freedom without responsibility, and they're offering freedom without reckoning. They are also offering *freedom without repercussions.* They're saying, "Oh, you can go out and do this, and there won't be any consequences. You can get away with it!" But you *can't* get away with it. "The wages of sin is death" (Rom. 6:23), and "the soul that sinneth, it shall die" (Ezek. 18:4). People who deliberately, repeatedly, lovingly, willingly live in sin are proving they have never been born again.

Freedom without Recession

They also offer *freedom without any recession*. They're saying, "This freedom gets better and better. As you enjoy sin, it gets better and better." But sin *doesn't* get better and better! It gets worse! Sin begins with a great deal of pleasure and ends with pain. Those who live in sin are in terrible bondage. They must have more and more sin, and yet they enjoy it less and less. Sin enslaves those who practice it.

Where False Freedom Leads

Peter gave us a third reason why we should avoid this false freedom—not only because of where it comes from and because of what it offers but *because of what it leads to.*

What does it lead to? Bondage. In 2 Peter 2:19 he said, "While they promised them liberty, they themselves are the servants of corruption; for of whom a man is overcome, of the same is he brought in bondage." They are entangled and overcome (v. 20). They want to use this doctrine of false freedom to get you into their cult, into their group, so they can make merchandise of you. They rob you. They exploit you. They ruin you. And it leads to bondage and to judgment.

I do not believe that any Christian will ever face eternal judgment. "There is, therefore, now no condemnation to them who are in Christ Jesus" (Rom. 8:1). But we may face terrible discipline in this life. In my ministry, I have met some people who have believed these false doctrines and have gotten into what they thought was freedom, and how God had to chasten them and discipline them! These false teachers bring upon themselves "swift destruction"

(2 Peter 2:1). They are reserved "unto the day of judgment" (v. 9). It is dangerous to get into false freedom because it leads to heartache, bondage, and discipline.

Peter illustrated this judgment by pointing to the angels (v. 4). Satan caused the fall of the angels, and where did they end up? In freedom? No! They ended up in bondage, in the chains of darkness.

In verse 5 he mentioned the world before the flood. People were living in freedom. They were enjoying life and ignoring God. Then judgment came! In verses 6–8 he pointed to Sodom and Gomorrah where people lived in the filthiness of the flesh. I don't have to elaborate on the horrible sins of Sodom and Gomorrah. Did those sins lead to freedom? They led to bondage! In verse 4 Satan led the angels astray. In verse 5 we have the world rejecting God. In verses 6–8 we have Sodom and Gomorrah, the flesh. In these verses we see the world, the flesh, and the Devil. If you live for the world, the flesh, and the Devil, you are living in a false freedom. It will only lead to bondage, discipline, and destruction.

Paul sounded the right note in Galatians 5:13: "For, brethren, ye have been called unto liberty; only use not liberty for an occasion to the flesh, but by love serve one another." This is the way we are supposed to live. True freedom is life controlled by truth and motivated by love. If you want to enjoy real freedom, serve other people in love. Sin's freedom is bondage, but bondage to Christ is true freedom. We should not use our liberty as an excuse to sin.

I want to warn you about this false freedom. Young Christians who have not yet been grounded in the Word of God need to be warned against those who want to make merchandise of them. The false teacher says, "You don't want to listen to the Word of God! You don't want to be identified with that Bible-preaching church! Come into our group. We have true freedom! You can enjoy the things of the world, the flesh, and the Devil, and you don't have to worry about responsibility or reckoning or reper- cussions!" They promise that life will get better and bet- ter, but in reality it will get worse and worse, and you will experience terrible chastening from the Lord. It is a dan- gerous thing to get involved in false freedom. Jesus said, "If the Son, therefore, shall make you free, ye shall be free indeed" (John 8:36). True freedom is life controlled by truth and motivated by love.

Are you involved in some false group, believing some false doctrine? Beware because all that is false will one day be cast into hell! Only what is true shall last. "And ye shall know the truth, and the truth shall make you free" (v. 32).

3

Freedom from Law

What does it mean to be free from the Law? "Stand fast, therefore, in the liberty with which Christ hath made us free, and be not entangled again with the yoke of bondage" (Gal. 5:1). What is freedom from the Law as far as the Christian is concerned? It certainly does not mean that Christians are permitted to be lawless. Rather it means that our relationship to God is not based on law but on grace.

Perhaps the best way to understand our freedom from the Law is to consider seven different pictures of the Law given to us in the New Testament. Each of these pictures tells us why the Law was given, what the Lord Jesus Christ did, and then what we must do in our relationship to Christ and to the Law.

The Law as a Yoke

In Galatians 5:1 we have the first picture of the Law: The Law is compared to *a yoke.* "Stand fast, therefore, in the liberty with which Christ hath made us free, and be not entangled again with the yoke of bondage." In Acts 15:10 we read: "Now, therefore, why put God to the test, to put a yoke upon the neck of the disciples, which neither our fathers nor we were able to bear?" The great question debated in Acts 15 was "Must a Gentile become a Jew to become a Christian?" Some of the legalists in the church said, "Yes, the Gentiles must put themselves under the Law," but the conclusion reached was "No, we must not put people under that yoke."

Why is the Law compared to a yoke? Who uses a yoke? Yokes are used with animals. The Law was given as a yoke to control us. Some tell us that people are basically good, that their problem is really the environment or the economy or education. No, each person is basically a sinner with a sinful nature, and that nature must be kept under control. One reason why God gave the Law was to control mankind. The Law never changes anybody; and in spite of the fact that we do have laws today, people still live like animals! But think of what the world would be like if there were no laws. As long as I am driving on the right side of the street, obeying the speed limit and doing what the law tells me to do, I have the freedom to drive. If I decide I want to drive on the wrong side of the street at twice the speed limit, I rob myself of freedom, and I need a yoke to control me. The Law was given to help control the sinful nature in people. God revealed His righteous judgments in the Law, and God warned us in the Law. But we still rebel against God.

The Lord Jesus Christ not only bore the yoke of the Law, but He bore the sins of the world on the cross. He fulfilled the Law. Galatians 5:1 tells us that we have been set free by the Lord Jesus Christ. When you're wearing a yoke, you are not standing straight on your feet. In order to wear a yoke, you would have to get down on all fours. The yoke burdens you, galls you, irritates you. The yoke is against you, but that yoke helps to control you.

Jesus Christ bore the curse of the Law when He died on the cross. Galatians 3:13 says, "Christ hath redeemed us from the curse of the law, being made a curse for us; for it is written, Cursed is everyone that hangeth on a tree." Instead of wearing the yoke of the Law, we Christians wear the wonderful yoke of Jesus Christ. He said in Matthew 11:28–30, "Come unto me, all ye that labor and are heavy laden, and I will give you rest. Take my yoke upon you, and learn of me; for I am meek and lowly in heart, and ye shall find rest unto your souls. For my yoke is easy, and my burden is light."

In other words, you and I as Christians have exchanged the *external* yoke of legalism for the *internal* yoke of love. We are related to Jesus Christ through a living, loving relationship, and we don't mind wearing His yoke because it is tailor-made for us. It is fitted to us. It is an easy yoke, and it helps us to be free. That is remarkable, isn't it? The yoke of the Law puts a person under bondage, but the yoke of Jesus Christ sets a person free. The yoke of the Law brought restlessness and agony, but the yoke of Jesus Christ brings rest to our souls. If you are a Christian, you are no longer to wear a yoke of the Law. That is bondage. Jesus bore your sins on the cross. Jesus fulfilled the righteous demands of the Law. Jesus was made a curse for you on the tree. Therefore, take His yoke, learn of Him, and enjoy the rest that He alone can give.

The Law as a Guardian

The second picture of the law is in Galatians 4:1–5: The Law is compared to *a guardian*. "Now I say that the heir, as long as he is a child, differeth nothing from a servant, though he be lord of all, but is under tutors and governors [guardians and stewards] until the time appointed of the father. Even so we, when we were children, were in bondage under the elements of the world. But, when the fullness of the time was come, God sent forth His Son, made of a woman, made under the law, to redeem them that were under the law, that we might receive the adoption of sons."

When Israel was called by God, it was like a nation of children. They were spiritually immature. You need guardians, tutors, and governors to take care of little children. In the Greek and Roman homes, slaves cared for the immature children. They took them to school and back and watched over them. The Law was like a guardian that watched over Israel during its immaturity.

When our children were small, we had to guard them. We had to have rules and regulations. Some things were very definitely off limits to our children. We would say, "Now, don't go near the highway" or "Don't go near the basement stairs" or "Don't leave the basement door open." Little children need guardians because they are immature and lack the discernment of adults.

When the Jewish nation came to its time of maturity, then the Savior, their Messiah, was sent to them. God wanted to usher them into a new relationship. He wanted to redeem them from the Law and give them the position of adult sons. "But, when the fullness of the time was come [the maturity of the nation], God sent forth His Son, made of a woman, made under the law, to redeem them that were under the law, that we might receive the adoption of sons" (vv. 4–5). The word "adoption" refers to "an adult standing in the family." Adults do not need guardians. Adults do not need servants and tutors to direct, protect, and care for them. Anyone who puts himself under the

Law is saying, "I want to be immature." It is impossible to mature if you put yourself under Law.

Christ has redeemed us from the law. We now have a position in the family as adult sons, not as little children. We no longer serve rules and regulations on the outside because we have the life of God on the inside. Galatians 4:6–7 says, "Because ye are sons, God hath sent forth the Spirit of his Son into your hearts, crying, Abba, Father. Wherefore, thou art no more a servant, but a son; and if a son, then an heir of God through Christ."

Jesus Christ died on the cross, rose again, and went back to heaven. He sent the Holy Spirit, and the Holy Spirit now lives in believers. We have the Spirit of God within; so we do not need the Law as a tutor, or a governor, on the outside. The Lord Jesus Christ has given us an adult standing in the family. It is a marvelous thing to know that you have an adult standing before God! God is not treating you like a little child. He has put His Spirit within you, and the Holy Spirit says, "Abba, Father." Our relationship to God is not that of a servant obeying laws; it is that of a son showing love, respect, and obedience.

The Law as a Slave Girl

In Galatians 4:21–31, the Law is pictured as *a slave girl.* This is the story of Abraham and Hagar from Genesis 16. You remember that Abraham got impatient waiting for his son to be born. Sarah suggested that Abraham take Hagar, her slave girl, as his wife. He did. A child, Ishmael, was born who turned out to be a real problem. When Isaac was born, a few years later, Ishmael persecuted Isaac and made trouble in the home. God said to Abraham, "Cast out the bondwoman and her son" (Gal. 4:30). The contrast here is between Sarah and Hagar: Sarah was a free woman, but Hagar was a slave. Sarah represents the heavenly Jerusalem, but Hagar represents the earthly Jerusalem in bondage.

Notice Galatians 4:24–26: "Which things are an allegory [a story that has hidden spiritual meaning], for these are the two covenants: the one from the Mount Sinai, bearing children for bondage, who is Hagar. For this Hagar is Mount Sinai in Arabia, and answereth to Jerusalem which now is, and is in bondage with her children. But Jerusalem which is above is free, which is the mother of us all." Hagar represents the earthly Jerusalem, the covenant of Law. Sarah represents the heavenly Jerusalem, the covenant of grace. Isaac was born a free son, but Ishmael was born a slave. Isaac represents our birth in the Spirit, and Ishmael represents our birth in the flesh.

When I was born the first time, I was born with a sinful nature and, like Ishmael, was a rebel, a troublemaker. When I was born again, I was born with a new nature (like the birth of Isaac) through the power of God. This new nature enables me to obey the Lord.

What did God say to Abraham? Galatians 4:30 says, "Cast out the bondwoman and her son; for the son of the bondwoman shall not be heir with the son of the freewoman." You cannot inherit anything through the Law. The only way to inherit anything from God is to be born into his family, and you cannot be born into his family through the Law. You must be born into the family through the power of the Holy Spirit. Abraham represents faith, and Sarah represents grace. Isaac, their son, was born by grace through faith. Abraham, Sarah, Isaac—these three represent the spiritual life. Hagar and Ishmael represent the old life, the life of bondage under law. We are not the children of the bondwoman but of the free woman. Your mother (spiritually) is not Hagar. The Law did not give you birth. The Spirit of God gave you your birth. Your mother, so to speak, is Sarah, the heavenly Jerusalem. You were born from above, born after the Spirit, born free, not

31

born into bondage. So the only thing we can do is cast out the bondwoman and her son.

When the Law goes, the power of the flesh has to go because "the strength of sin is the law" (1 Cor. 15:56). When the Law says, "Don't do this!" my old nature says, "I'm going to do it!" When the Law says, "You'd better do that!" I say, "Oh, no I won't!" The old nature *knows* no law, but the new nature *needs* no law. We are not under the bondage of the Law. We were not born as slave children. We were born free. We were born under grace, and therefore, we are no longer under the bondage of the Law.

Abraham was never supposed to marry Hagar. God never married the Law to grace. The Law has its function. It tells me I need grace, convicts me of sin, and tells me that God is righteous and that sin leads to death. But Abraham was never supposed to marry Hagar, and so God said, "Cast out the bondwoman and her son" (Gal. 4:30). We are not under the yoke of the Law. We are wearing the yoke of Christ. We no longer need guardians or babysitters because we have the Spirit within. We are adult sons in the family. We are not related to the slave girl, Hagar. We are free because we have been born again by the Spirit of the living God.

4

Freedom from Law (cont.)

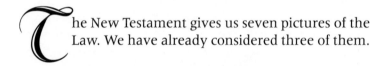he New Testament gives us seven pictures of the Law. We have already considered three of them.

The Law as a Bond of Indebtedness

In Colossians 2:14 we have a fourth picture of the Law: *the bond of indebtedness.* If you have ever owed anybody money, you know something about the bond of indebtedness. Paul was writing about the work of Jesus Christ on the cross: "Blotting out the handwriting of ordinances that was against us, which was contrary to us, and took it out of the way, nailing it to His cross." We were in debt to the Law.

The Law was against us. You must remember that the Law was not given to save people. It was given to show people they needed to be saved. The Law was against us because it revealed sin. It was against us because it revealed the holy and righteous judgments of God. The Law was not only against us, but it was also contrary to us. This takes us a step further, doesn't it? We *could not* obey it. No matter how much we try, we cannot fully obey the Law.

You may say, "I have never murdered anybody." I'm glad for that, but Jesus said that if you hate someone in your heart, you have committed murder in your heart. We may say, "Well, I have never bowed down before an idol." That may be true, but is Jesus Christ *first* in your life? Are there other gods demanding your allegiance and your obedience? What are you sacrificing to today? It is possible for us to outwardly conform to the standards of the Law but inwardly be committing all kinds of sin. The Law is not only *against* us, but the Law is *contrary* to us.

The Law itself is "holy, and just, and good" (Rom. 7:12). Nowhere does the Bible say that the Law is bad. *We* are the ones who are bad. If that which is holy and just and good shows us how bad we are, then we really must be bad! God does not have to use *bad* things to show us how bad we are. He uses *good* things—such as the Law—to show us how bad we are! This shows us the extent of the depravity of the human heart!

So you and I had a bond of indebtedness that we could not pay. We were totally bankrupt. The Lord Jesus told a parable about two men (see Luke 7:40–50). One owed 500 denarii and the other owed 50 denarii. (One denarius equaled a day's wages.) Neither could pay, but the banker graciously forgave both of them! You and I were completely bankrupt before God. Sinners may not think they are bankrupt. They may think they are rich. But in the sight of God, we are poor and wretched and blind and naked. We have nothing in ourselves. Our righteousness is like filthy rags (see Isa. 64:6). We cannot begin to conform to the standards of God. So what did Jesus do? He paid the debt for us. He blotted out the handwriting of ordinances (Col. 2:14). In other words, he cancelled the debt. In Paul's day legal documents were written on parchment and vellum. You could use water or some other fluid to erase, expunge, wash away completely the writing that was on the document.

When Jesus died for us on the cross, He not only washed away the writing on the document, but He also nailed the document to his cross. He took it out of the way. Some people today want to put the Law back into the center of their lives. When Jesus died on the cross, He tore the veil of the temple in two. This signified that there was no longer any separation between man and God. We can come through the blood of Jesus Christ to our Father in heaven. The way is open. All the ceremonies have been fulfilled, every demand of the Law has been met, every debt has been paid. He also knocked down the middle wall of partition between Jew and Gentile (see Eph. 2:14). There are no more racial distinctions. The Law that was given to the Jews was never given to the Gentiles. That racial distinction has been completely erased.

Jesus blotted out the handwriting of ordinances that was against us. We are no longer in debt! He has taken it out of the way. The Law is no longer the central thing in our lives. What is the central thing? The cross. Paul said, "God forbid that I should glory, except in the cross of our Lord Jesus Christ" (Gal. 6:14). Why do we obey God? Because of the Law that is hanging over our head? No. *Because of a life that is within our heart.* Our debt, or responsibility, is not to fulfill the Law. Our debt is to love. Romans 13:8 says, "Owe no man any thing, but to love one another; for he that loveth another hath fulfilled the law." Colossians 2:14 affirms that the bond of indebtedness has been erased and has been nailed to the cross, and therefore, we owe no debt to the Law. Does this mean we are lawless? Of course not! It means that the Law is now written in our hearts because we have the Holy Spirit within. A new nature within gives us the desire and the

35

power to obey God and to live up to the righteous standards of the Law.

The Law as a Shadow

As we continue in Colossians 2, we discover a fifth picture of the Law: *the shadows.* Colossians 2:16–17 says, "Let no man, therefore, judge you in food, or in drink, or in respect of a feast day, or of the new moon, or of a Sabbath day, which are a shadow of things to come; but the body is of Christ."

The problem in Colossae was this: the Christians were being taught by false teachers who mixed Law and grace. They taught that believers had to obey the Old Testament dietary laws and observe the yearly feasts. Paul wrote, in effect: "Don't let them judge you in respect to a holy day (the annual feasts) or the new moon (the monthly celebration) or the Sabbath Day (the weekly celebration)" (v. 16). All of these special days were a part of the "shadow of things to come" (v. 17).

The same truth is taught in Hebrews 10:1: "For the law, having a shadow of good things to come and not the very image of the things, can never with those sacrifices which they offered year by year continually make those who come to it perfect." The Law is simply a shadow. Heavenly, spiritual realities are pictured in earthly, physical copies. The tabernacle was a copy of God's tabernacle in heaven. The sacrifices were a copy of the sacrifice of Jesus Christ. When you put yourself under the Law, you are going from the light into the shadows. When you put yourself under the Law, you are exchanging the reality for the copy. This would be like a new bride's expressing love to a picture of her husband and ignoring the man himself. It would be like having a son or daughter show great admiration and adoration for a picture of their mother and father and not showing love to their actual parents.

These things are "a shadow of things to come; but the body [the fulfillment] is of Christ" (Col. 2:17). Shadows don't last. Shadows are cast when light shines from behind some solid object. The false teachers thought that feast days, Sabbath days, and the dietary laws were the reality. Actually they were only the shadows that pointed to the reality. All reality is in Jesus Christ. He is the truth. He is the Word. God has wrapped up in Jesus Christ all the reality that we will ever need. He has fulfilled the Law. Therefore, we are living in the light and not in the shadows. When we place ourselves under the Law, not only are we putting ourselves under a yoke of bondage, not only are we making ourselves a child (cared for by a guardian), not only are we putting ourselves into slavery and under a bond of indebtedness, but also we are putting ourselves back in the shadows.

The Law as a Mirror

In James 1 gives a sixth picture of the Law: It is compared to *a mirror.* James 1:22–25 says, "But be ye doers of the word and not hearers only, deceiving your own selves. For if any be a hearer of the word, and not a doer, he is like a man beholding his natural face in a mirror; for he beholdeth himself, and goeth his way, and immediately forgetteth what manner of man he was. But whosoever looketh into the perfect law of liberty, and continueth in it, he being not a forgetful hearer but a doer of the work, this man shall be blessed in his deed." The law is a mirror that reveals sin. You look into the mirror and see that your face is dirty, *but you don't wash your face in the mirror!* The mirror shows you that you are dirty, but the mirror cannot cleanse you. The Law is God's mirror to show us how dirty we are. When I read the Word of God, I realize that I am a sinner and therefore need a Savior.

When you know Jesus Christ as your Savior, the Word of God becomes your mirror, according to 2 Corinthians 3:18: "But we all, with unveiled face beholding as in a mirror the glory of the Lord, are changed into the same image from glory to glory, even as by the Spirit of the Lord." When the child of God looks into the Word of God (the mirror) and sees the Son of God, he is transformed by the Spirit of God into the image of God for the glory of God. The Law never changed anybody; it is only a mirror that shows us our sin. When you have Jesus Christ as your Savior and the Holy Spirit lives within you, the Word becomes a mirror that transforms you from glory to glory. You become more like the Lord Jesus Christ! If you put yourself under the Law, all you can do is look in the mirror and see how dirty you are. That creates guilt and condemnation, but it never changes you for the better. It always changes you for the worse.

The Law as a Husband

Our final picture of the Law is in Romans 7:1–4: It is compared to *a husband.*

> Know ye not, brethren (for I speak to them that know the law), how that the law hath dominion over a man as long as he liveth? For the woman who hath an husband is bound by the law to her husband as long as he liveth; but if the husband be dead, she is loosed from the law of her husband. So, then if, while her husband liveth, she be married to another man, she shall be called an adulteress; but if her husband be dead, she is free from that law, so that she is no adulteress, though she be married to another man. Wherefore, my brethren, ye also are become dead to the law by the body of Christ, that ye should be mar-

ried to another, even to him who is raised from the dead, that we should bring forth fruit unto God.

When a woman marries a man, she has a permanent, binding obligation. Israel was wedded to the Law. At Sinai, they had agreed to obey the Law. The Law was like a husband, giving directions to them and being in dominion over them. The interesting thing is this: Paul did not say that the husband died; he said that *we* died. The Law is not dead. The Law is very much alive. The Law is holy and just and good. We are the sinners. We are the ones who died. We have a new relationship to the Law because we have died. When Jesus died, we died with Him. When He arose, we arose with Him. Therefore, we are dead to the Law.

The Law is not dead to us. If you put yourself back under the Law, you will discover how powerful the Law is to condemn. But when you have been saved through Jesus Christ, you are united to Him in His death, burial, and resurrection. This means you have died to the Law. You have been raised to walk in newness of life. You are married, not to the Law but to Jesus Christ. Your relationship is one of love and life, not one of Law.

Paul used marriage as an illustration of our relationship to the Law: "But now we are delivered from the law, that being dead in which we were held, that we should serve in newness of spirit and not in the oldness of the letter" (v. 6). Can you imagine a husband's putting up a list of rules and regulations in order to control his wife? No! How do a husband and wife build a happy home? Through a loving, living, growing relationship. You are married to Jesus Christ. You have His name. You share His wealth. One day you will live in His home. You enjoy His love. You have His protection. You share His future. We are married to Jesus Christ. We are not married to the Law. We died to the Law. We have been delivered from the Law.

Therefore, we can walk in newness of life and serve in newness of the Spirit because we don't have a relationship of obligation and galling responsibility. We have a loving, living relationship to a wonderful Savior, and He is our husband.

How wonderful it is to be united to Jesus Christ in life and in love but not in Law. We obey Him, not because we fear Him but because we love Him. We obey Him, not because He holds threats over our heads but because He blesses us.

To review these seven pictures: We are no longer under the yoke of the law, controlled by guardians, related to slave girls, owing a bond of indebtedness. We are not in the shadows. We are not looking in a mirror that makes us look dirty. We are not married to a domineering husband. No, we have a wonderful, living relationship with the Lord Jesus Christ! We are free from the Law, free to live for Him.

5

Freedom from Sin

*E*very Christian has to battle with three enemies: the world, the flesh, and the Devil. These three enemies come from our old life. In Ephesians 2:1–3 Paul described our old life: "And you hath he made alive, who were dead in trespasses and sins; in which in times past ye walked according to the course of this world [there is the world], according to the prince of the power of the air, the spirit that now worketh in the sons of disobedience [there is the Devil]; among whom also we all had our manner of life in times past in the lusts of our flesh [there is the flesh]."

Before I was a Christian, I lived according to the dictates of this world. I was controlled by the power of Satan, and I lived to satisfy the desires of the flesh. When I became a Christian, I was set free from these enemies, but they are still enemies! They still want to attack me and defeat me. You and I face a struggle to overcome these enemies. It's wonderful to know that Jesus Christ has made provision for us to have victory. Through Jesus Christ, we can have freedom from the sins of the flesh. This is not to say that we can live perfectly sinless lives, because "if we say that we have no sin, we deceive ourselves, and the truth is not in us" (1 John 1:8). But it is possible for us to live in victory over deliberate sin if we will simply follow the instructions that God gives to us in Romans 6.

The theme of Romans 6 is how to stop doing bad things, how to live in victory over the flesh. In this chapter Paul gave three very simple instructions: know, reckon, and yield. In the first ten verses he talked about what we should *know*. Then in verse 11 he said we should *reckon* on what we know, and in verses 12–23 he told us we should *yield*. He gave instruction to the mind: *know*. Then he gave instruction to the heart: *reckon*. Finally, he gave instruction to the will: *yield*.

What We Should Know

In the first three chapters of Romans, Paul dealt with the topic of sin and concluded that the whole world stands condemned before God. What, then, is the answer? The answer is salvation through faith in Jesus Christ, and this he discussed in Romans 4 and 5. In chapter 4 he referred to Abraham and showed that Abraham was saved the same way everybody else has to be saved—by faith. In chapter 5 he went all the way back to Adam and pointed out that we are in the mess we are in because of Adam's fall. In Adam we all fell; in Christ we can be made alive again.

At this point somebody might raise some objections. (There are always those who raise objections!) Paul said, "But where sin abounded, grace did much more abound" (v. 20). "If we are saved by grace through faith apart from works," says the objector, "why don't we just continue in sin that grace may abound? The more we sin, the more God's grace will abound, and the more God will be glorified!"

I often hear from people who do not believe in the doctrine of "the perseverance of the saints"; that is, that once you are saved, you are saved forever. They write to me and say, "Brother Wiersbe, if you tell people they are saved forever, they'll go out and sin!" This is the objection that Paul dealt with in Romans 6. He said that we need to know three fundamental truths. We need to know something about sin, something about the work of Christ on the cross, and something about ourselves.

About Sin

We need to know something about sin. What did Paul say about sin in this chapter? He said that *sin enslaves.* Sin always begins with freedom, but it leads to slavery. You may be playing with sin right now, or you may be contemplating sin. You are a believer in Jesus Christ, but perhaps ideas of sin are lingering in the back of your mind. I want to warn you that sin enters as a *guest;* then sin becomes a *friend*—you get to know each other and like each other. Then sin becomes a *servant.* It promises to serve you and to give you pleasure. But that servant becomes a *master,* that master becomes a *tyrant,* and that tyrant becomes a *destroyer.* Sin always begins with freedom and ends with destruction and slavery.

"For we ourselves also were once foolish, disobedient, deceived, serving various lusts and pleasures, living in malice and envy, hateful, and hating one another" (Titus 3:3). That's the way it was before we were born again. People have the idea that sin is serving them, but they are wrong. They are serving sin! Paul told us very clearly that Christians are "freed from sin" (Rom. 6:7) and "should not serve

43

sin" (v. 6). You and I need to deal drastically with sin. That's the first thing Paul wanted us to know. He wanted us to know that sin is a terrible tyrant that will dominate our life, if we permit it.

About Christ's Work

Second, *he wanted us to know something about Christ's work on the cross.*

> How shall we, that are dead to sin, live any longer in it? Know ye not that, as many of us as were baptized into Jesus Christ were baptized into his death? Therefore, we are buried with him by baptism into death, that as Christ was raised up from the dead by the glory of the Father, even so we also should walk in newness of life. For if we have been planted together in the likeness of his death, we shall be also in the likeness of his resurrection; knowing this, that our old man is crucified with him, that the body of sin might be destroyed, that henceforth we should not serve sin. For he that is dead is freed from sin. Now if we be dead with Christ, we believe that we shall also live with him, knowing that Christ, being raised from the dead, dieth no more; death hath no more dominion over him. For in that he died, he died unto sin once; but in that he liveth, he liveth unto God.
>
> Romans 6:2–10

There is a contrast in emphasis between Romans 5 and Romans 6. In Romans 5 Paul dealt with *substitution*—Christ died for me, but in Romans 6 he dealt with *identification*— I died with Him. In Romans 5 Paul said that Jesus died *for* sin, but in Romans 6 he said that Jesus died *unto* sin. What's the difference? According to chapter 5 Jesus Christ died to deal with the *penalty* of sin, but according to chapter 6 Jesus Christ died to break the *power* of sin. Chapter 5 deals with justification, our standing before God. Chapter 6 deals with sanctification, our victory through the Lord Jesus Christ. We have an entirely new relationship with sin because of the work of the Lord Jesus Christ.

When you trusted Jesus Christ as your Savior, the Holy Spirit of God baptized you into the Body of Christ. This baptism did not occur after conversion but was simultaneous with conversion (1 Cor. 12:13; Eph. 1:13 NASB). Every believer has the gift of the Holy Spirit, and every believer has been identified with Jesus Christ in His death, burial, resurrection, and ascension. This is the beautiful truth of Romans 6. This is why Paul said, "What shall we say then? Shall we continue in sin, that grace may abound? God forbid" (vv. 1–2). After all we have experienced in Jesus Christ, how can we continue in sin?

To begin with, we are *dead to sin* (v. 2). According to Romans 6:7, the old man is crucified: "For he that is dead is freed from sin." Sin is not dead to me, but *I am dead to sin.* Sin is very much alive, but we are dead to sin because we have been buried with Christ and raised up to newness of life. We have been crucified with Christ.

We have been freed from sin. "Being, then, made free from sin, ye became the servants of righteousness" (v. 18). "But now being made free from sin, and become servants to God, ye have your fruit unto holiness, and the end everlasting life" (v. 22).

Please understand your new position in Jesus Christ. When Jesus died, you died in Him and with Him. When He was buried, your old life was buried in Him and with Him. When He arose, you arose with Him in newness of life. You are in Jesus Christ, and you have a new relationship to sin. You are dead to sin. The old man has been crucified. You are freed from sin, and therefore, you have the privilege of living in victory over sin.

45

About Yourself

Third, *you need to know something about yourself.* You must choose your master. A famous British preacher, Dr. P. T. Forsyth, used to say that our purpose in life is not to find our freedom but to find our master. When you find the right master, then you will have the right kind of freedom. If sin is your master, then you will serve sin and have a life of defeat, despair, disappointment, and emptiness. But if Jesus Christ is your Master, then you will have a life of victory, a life of vitality. You can walk in newness of life, in a marvelous life of joy and victory. You have to choose your master.

What We Should Reckon

Paul went on to say in Romans 6:11, "Likewise, reckon ye also yourselves to be dead indeed unto sin, but alive unto God through Jesus Christ, our Lord." Nineteen times in the book of Romans he used the Greek word *logizomai* that is translated "reckoned." Sometimes it is translated "impute" or "count." This is the second instruction that he gives: *reckon.*

What does it mean to reckon? To reckon means to rely on, to claim for yourself that which God says is true in the Bible. Suppose that I owed you $25 and that I wrote you a check and mailed it to you. You say, "My, but this is a beautiful check! What a lovely picture on the check!" You put the check in your pocket, and you never cash it. You are not reckoning. But when you go to the bank and endorse the check, you are reckoning. You are saying, "I believe that what Wiersbe has said on this check is true. I believe there is money in the bank; therefore, I am going to cash the check."

How do you know that you died with Jesus Christ on the cross? The Bible says you did. If I were to ask you,

"How many crosses were on Calvary?" you would say, "Three." Jesus was in the middle, and two thieves were on either side. How do you know this? How do you know that there were two thieves with Jesus on Calvary? Because the Bible says so. Well, the same Bible that says two thieves died with Jesus *also says that you died with Jesus!* If you really believe the one, you have to believe the other. To reckon simply means to believe that what the Word says is true—true in *my* life.

Reckoning is not trying to work up an experience. I find saints who are always trying to work up an experience. Reckoning is simply believing that what God said in Romans 6 is true. Sin is not dead to me, but I am dead to sin. I am not trying to work up an emotional experience. I am simply believing what God said. That's reckoning. Reckoning simply means that I am acting in faith. I am united with Jesus Christ. God's Word is true. The work of Christ is completed. Therefore, what God says in the Word is true in my life.

Are you reckoning yourself to be dead indeed unto sin (that's the negative) but alive unto God through Jesus Christ our Lord (that's the positive)? The key word here is the word "Lord." Jesus Christ is not just our Savior, but He is also our Lord. Are you reckoning on this?

Let me review what we have studied. The first instruction Paul gave in Romans 6 is *know.* We should know something about sin (it enslaves us), about the work of Christ (He has freed us), about ourselves (we must choose our master). His second instruction was *reckon.* This is the work of the heart, believing for myself that what God says in the Word is true in my life. Now for the third instruction.

6

Freedom from Sin (cont.)

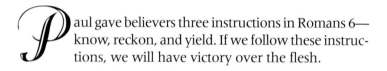aul gave believers three instructions in Romans 6—know, reckon, and yield. If we follow these instructions, we will have victory over the flesh.

What We Should Yield

Paul's third instruction in Romans 6 was *yield.* "Let not sin, therefore, reign in your mortal body, that ye should obey it in its lusts" (v. 12). A distinction is made between *sin* and *the body.* Once in a while I receive mail from radio listeners asking whether or not the body is sinful. No, the body is not sinful. The body is neutral. But a force at work within the body (which the Bible calls the flesh, the old man) wants us to use our body in a sinful way. In verse 12 of Romans 6, Paul began with a word addressed to my will: "Let not." My mind must *know* the truth, my heart must *reckon* on this truth, but my will must *act* on this truth.

"Let not sin, therefore, reign in your mortal body, that ye should obey it in its lusts."

Sin comes in as a guest and then becomes a friend. Then the friend becomes a servant, and the servant becomes a master. You think you are controlling sin, but sin is controlling you. "Neither yield ye your members [the parts of your body] as instruments of unrighteousness unto sin" (v. 13). The Greek word translated "instruments" means weapons. It also can be applied to tools. My hands, my feet, my tongue—the various parts of my body—can be used by sin to do unrighteousness, or they can be used by God to do righteousness. The body itself is neutral. *The master* makes the difference. If sin is your master, then you will live in unrighteousness. If Christ is your Master, then you will live in holiness. "But yield yourselves unto God, as those that are alive from the dead, and your members as instruments of righteousness unto God" (v. 13).

Paul was talking about a living sacrifice, one who is "alive from the dead." Our Lord Jesus Christ is in heaven today with a glorified body. He is a living sacrifice, for he bears the marks of Calvary on that glorified body. The only works of man in heaven today that I know of are the wounds on the body of the Lord Jesus. Jesus is a living sacrifice. In the Old Testament Isaac was a living sacrifice. Isaac yielded himself to his father and willingly put himself on the altar. He was bound and, to all intents and purposes, was slain. God stopped Abraham from killing his son. But as far as God was concerned, Isaac died and was (in a type) raised from the dead. Isaac was freed and became a living sacrifice.

Paul applied this same truth in Romans 12:1–2. These verses are so familiar that sometimes we overlook them or take them for granted. The Greek word translated "yield" in Romans 6 *(paristēmi)* is the same word translated "present" in Romans 12:1. "I beseech you therefore,

49

brethren, by the mercies of God, that ye present your bodies a living sacrifice, holy, acceptable unto God, which is your reasonable service."

Our Bodies

God wants you to give Him your body. That sounds very ordinary, but it's one of the most spiritual things you can do! If God is going to use you, He must have your body. When Jesus Christ came to earth to redeem us, He had to have a body. In order to get His message of salvation to a wicked world, Jesus Christ must have a Body—the Church. God can use my fingers to write letters. He can use my feet to make visits in homes. He can use my lips to speak the message of truth. That's why you should take good care of your body—it's the only tool you've got. A person would be a fool to pour sand into his gas tank, wouldn't he? He would wreck the car. Well, people do some foolish things with their bodies. God wants your body as a holy sacrifice, as a complete sacrifice to Him. Just as Jesus gave His body on the cross for you, God wants you to give your body on the altar for Him.

Our Minds

Paul went on to say in Romans 12:2, "But be ye transformed by the renewing of your mind." Not only should I give God my body, but *I should also give him my mind.* Why? Because my mind controls my body. What you think about is what you do. You say, "Well, I've thought about things I've never done." If you keep thinking about them long enough, you'll do them! "As he thinketh in his heart, so he is," says Proverbs 23:7. "Be not conformed to this world" (Rom. 12:2). Don't think the way the world thinks. "Blessed is the man who walketh not in the counsel of the ungodly, nor standeth in the way of sinners, nor sitteth in the seat of the scornful" (Ps. 1:1).

Our Wills

"Be not conformed to this world, but be ye transformed by the renewing of your mind, that ye may prove what is that good, and acceptable, and perfect, will of God" (Rom. 12:2). *God also wants my will.* God wants you to yield your body, your mind, and your will to Him. He wants you to do this because you love Him. He wants your heart. Because of all that God has done for you, you should gladly yield yourself to Him.

Results of Yielding

When we yield ourselves to God, a wonderful thing happens: *We get victory over sin!* "For sin shall not have dominion over you; for ye are not under the law but under grace" (Rom. 6:14). What does the Law have to do with victory? According to 1 Corinthians 15:56, "The strength of sin is the law." Romans 7 teaches us that the very law that tells me what I should not do arouses in me the desire to do it. The Law is good, but I am sinful. The Law never changed a person's nature. The Law cannot control sin, and it cannot change sinners. What does the Law do? It reveals sin. "The strength of sin is the law." The minute you say to a child, "Don't do that!" he starts figuring out some way to do it. Why? Because he has a nature within that does not want to obey the Law. "What then? Shall we sin, because we are not under the Law, but under grace? God forbid" (6:15).

You and I must yield ourselves to God. Then He becomes the master of our lives. We give Him our body, our mind, our will, our heart. We allow the Word of God to trans-

51

form our minds, and as He transforms our minds by His Word, He guides us by His Spirit, and we become the servants of God. It is a beautiful thing to be set free from this old life and to walk in what the Bible calls "newness of life." "But God be thanked, that whereas ye were the servants of sin, ye have obeyed from the heart that form of doctrine which was delivered you. Being, then, made free from sin, ye became the servants of righteousness" (vv. 17–18).

Paul applied this in verses 19 and 20: "I speak after the manner of men [I'm using a human illustration] because of the infirmity of your flesh; for as ye have yielded your members servants to uncleanness and to iniquity, unto iniquity [when you were lost, you yielded the parts of your body to sin]; even so now yield your members servants to righteousness, unto holiness. For when ye were the servants of sin, ye were free from righteousness." That's a terrible freedom, isn't it? We were in the bondage of sin, and we couldn't perform righteous deeds. Now we are in Jesus Christ, righteous in Him; therefore, we can be free from sin.

Paul asked an important question in verse 21: "What fruit had ye then in those things of which ye are now ashamed?" Think about that. Have you ever said, "I would like to go back to my old life"? I hope not! What was the blessing of your old life? Have you forgotten what it was like to be in bondage to sin? The next time you're tempted to go back into the world or to serve the flesh, just remember what you were before. In Deuteronomy God told the Jews to remind themselves regularly that they were once in bondage in Egypt. The trouble was that when the Israelites thought about Egypt, they thought only about the leeks and the onions and the garlic. They remembered the good things. They forgot their taskmasters, their chains, and their bondage. "What fruit had ye then in those things of which ye are now ashamed? For the end of those things is death. But now being made free from sin, and become servants to God [yielding yourself to God], ye have your fruit unto holiness, and the end everlasting life" (Rom. 6:21–22). What a marvelous thing—to produce fruit unto holiness, to have a fruitful life! Now that we are in Jesus Christ and yielded to him, we can produce fruit!

"For the wages of sin is death" (v. 23). Paul didn't write this verse to unbelievers in a rescue mission. He wrote Romans 6:23 to believers in a local assembly. Samson discovered the wages of sin. When a Christian plays around with sin, sin becomes his master, then sin becomes his tyrant, and then sin becomes his destroyer. King Saul discovered that. There were Christians in Corinth who had sinned, and God had to take their lives. "There is a sin unto death," we're told in 1 John 5:16. If you work for sin, you'll receive the wages that sin pays, and the wages of sin is death. But if you are working for God, if you have yielded yourself to God, "The gift of God is eternal life through Jesus Christ, our Lord" (Rom. 6:23). Take your choice.

Know. Know what? Know that sin enslaves. Know that Jesus Christ has set you free from this slavery and that you must choose your master.

Reckon. Reckon that what God says in His Word is true. Believe it for yourself.

Yield. Present your body, your mind, your will, your heart to God. Let the Holy Spirit work in your life to overcome the flesh and to produce fruit unto God. This means a daily yielding. It sometimes means a struggle against sin. We are not talking about some once-for-all decision that puts you on such a high plane that you will never again be tempted. You may have some occasional falls. Then you get up and say, "Lord, I'm sorry, forgive me." He forgives you, and you get going again.

"The victorious Christian life," said Alexander Whyte, "is a series of new beginnings." As you spend time in the Word of God and prayer, as you fellowship with other Christians, you find yourself growing in your Christian freedom. When Jesus died for you, He died not only to rescue you from the *penalty* of sin, which is eternal death, but He died to rescue you from the very *power* of sin. My prayer is that all of us might experience this beautiful life of fruitfulness and freedom to the glory of God. The Lord Jesus Christ did not die to make me a slave. He died to make me a son.

I would urge you to meditate on Romans 6 and to notice these three simple instructions: *know, reckon, yield.* Then yield yourself daily to the Lord. Your freedom in Christ will make you free from sin, and you will have victory over the Tempter to the glory of God.

7

Freedom from People

$\mathcal{I}$t is dangerous when spiritual leaders become dictators and we become enslaved to people. "Not that we have dominion over your faith," wrote the Apostle Paul, "but are helpers of your joy" (2 Cor. 1:24). In 1 Corinthians 7:17–24 Paul laid down a basic principle that we should not be subject to people.

But as God hath distributed to every man, as the Lord hath called every one, so let him walk. And so ordain I in all churches. Is any man called being circumcised? Let him not become uncircumcised. Is any called in uncircumcision? Let him not be circumcised. Circumcision is nothing, and uncircumcision is nothing, but the keeping of the commandments of God. Let every man abide in the same calling in which he was called. Art thou called, being a servant? Care not for it; but if thou mayest be made free, use it rather. For he that is called in the Lord, being a servant, is the Lord's freeman; likewise also he that is called, being free, is Christ's servant. Ye are bought with a price; be not

ye the servants of men. Brethren, let every man, in whatever state he is called, there abide with God.

1 Corinthians 7:17–24

Let's consider this subject of freedom from people from
three different aspects.

The Setting

First of all, consider *the setting.* If we don't understand
the setting of this passage, we are going to make some false
interpretations. Paul was having problems with the Corinthians because of their abuse of their new freedom. The
Corinthian church was comprised of people some of whom
had lived in gross sin. Many of them had been involved
in very wicked practices, and now they had freedom in
the Lord Jesus Christ.

Galatians 3:28 is the key that will help us in studying
this chapter: "There is neither Jew nor Greek, there is neither bond nor free, there is neither male nor female; for
ye are all one in Christ Jesus." The Corinthian believers
knew that truth, but they were taking it to the extreme.
They were making use of their freedom to the point of
license.

For example, they said, "When you are saved and in
Jesus Christ, there is neither male nor female; so that abol-
ishes our marriages." In 1 Corinthians 7:1–16 Paul explained
the Christian marriage relationship. When a person becomes
a Christian, it does not abolish his marriage relationship.
Rather it gives new potential for victory and blessing in that
marriage relationship. The women in the Corinthian church
were carrying their freedom a little bit too far, but so were
the men.

"There is neither Jew nor Greek" (Gal. 3:28). Paul dealt
with this in 1 Corinthians 7:17–20. The Jews who got

saved wanted to become like the Gentiles and tried to erase the mark of the covenant from their body. On the other hand, the Gentiles wanted to become like the Jews! There is neither Jew nor Gentile in Jesus Christ, but this does not erase one's nationality. When I was saved, my nationality did not change.

"There is neither bond nor free" (Gal. 3:28). He dealt with this in 1 Corinthians 7:21–24. Some slaves who had been saved said, "We are no longer slaves! We don't have to obey our masters anymore!" Paul wrote to them and said, "You had better be careful how you use your freedom." They were tempted to make changes that God never meant to be made. He did tell the slaves that if an opportunity came along for freedom, they should use it. But they were to use it for the glory of God, not for their own selfish purposes.

In Jesus Christ "There is neither male nor female" (Gal. 3:28); but when you were saved, your sex did not change. In Jesus Christ there is neither Jew nor Gentile; but when you were saved, your racial or national origins did not change. In Jesus Christ there is neither bond nor free; but when you were saved, your economic or social status did not change. Salvation gives us the potential to make the most out of every situation. Salvation is a *spiritual* change. It can bring about changes in the home, on the job, and in society. But God doesn't work from the outside in; He works from the inside out. Paul was very careful to tell those people that their freedom in Jesus Christ must not be abused and turned into license.

The Meaning

Let's look now at *the meaning* of the passage. Paul laid down a fundamental principle here that he gave in all churches; namely, *remain as you are, and let God make the changes.*

"But as God hath distributed to every man, as the Lord hath called every one, so let him walk. . . . Let every man abide in the same calling in which he was called. . . . Brethren, let every man, in whatever state he is called, there abide with God" (1 Cor. 7:17, 20, 24). Remain as you are. Don't try to make a lot of radical changes immediately. Allow the changes to come from within. Paul reminded us that we are free, but we are not independent. No Christian can be independent of other Christians. *But no Christian must be dependent on others.* That is, no pastor should be a spiritual dictator in the lives of the people. No Sunday school teacher should be a spiritual dictator in the lives of the class members. Jesus warned us not to call any person on earth our spiritual father (see Matt. 23:8–12). There is a sense in which those who lead us to Christ are our spiritual fathers (1 Cor. 4:15), but not in the sense of being dictators over our lives. The slaves were to consider themselves free in Christ, but they were still slaves. The masters were to consider themselves Christ's slaves, but they were still masters. You are free from the domination of people, but this does not make you independent. This should not cause you to make all sorts of radical changes. Allow the changes to come from within.

We Are Called by God

Paul presented four arguments to prove that we should remain as we are and let God make the changes from within. First, *we are called by God.* "As the Lord hath called every one" (1 Cor. 7:17). This idea is repeated in verses 18, 20, 21, 22, and 24. In fact, he used the words "called" and "calling" nine times in this passage. He concluded the passage: "Brethren, let every man, in whatever state he is

called, there abide with God" (v. 24). This does not mean
that if you are offered a promotion on your job, you should
turn it down. He was saying that, because you are a Christian, you don't try to make a lot of radical changes. Let
God do the changing. You have been called by God.

We Have Been Assigned by God

First Corinthians 7:17 says, "As God hath distributed to
every man." The word "distributed" means "assigned to
him." Our place in society, our job, our gifts are assignments
from God. This is Paul's second argument. You have been
called by God, and *you have been assigned by God.* Some slave
may say, "I can't see how being a slave is a gift from God!"
That is not for us to argue or debate. God knows what He
is doing, and when God wants to make the changes, they
will be made. We should not run around trying to make all
sorts of radical changes just because we are Christians. That
does not mean we should not try to better our condition.
Nobody wants to remain in a difficult situation. But if this
is the place that God assigned, we have to accept it as His
will until He changes it. However, as Paul said to the slaves,
if the opportunity for improvement comes, make use of it.
But be sure the changes come from God.

We Belong to God

The third argument is given in 1 Corinthians 7:23: "Ye
are bought with a price; be not ye the servants of men."
You belong to God. The value of an object is measured by
the price you pay for it. It's amazing what some people
will pay for certain objects. Jesus Christ shed His blood for
us! That shows how valuable we are to God. "Ye are bought
with a price." You belong to God, He purchased you.
Therefore, "be not ye the servants of men." The servant

serves the one who purchased him. We have been purchased by Jesus Christ; so we must serve Him.

We Should Abide with God

In 1 Corinthians 7:24 Paul gave a fourth argument: "Let every man . . . abide with God." *We are to abide with God.* If you are where God has placed you, doing the job God has given you to do, you are abiding with God. If you rebel against God's will, you will not abide with God. If we don't abide with God, we cannot bear spiritual fruit. And so his argument is simply this: Remain as you are. Let God make the changes because he assigns us our ministry in life.

The Application

The third aspect of freedom from people is *living it.* How can you and I practically apply this truth in our lives?

I fear that many people are under bondage to others. They live in fear of other people. Proverbs 29:25 says that the fear of men brings a snare. We must not be independent of people. We must never say, "I don't care how they feel or what they think." *We must care,* but we must not be subservient. We must not be enslaved to the opinions of others.

I face this problem week in and week out. People phone or write and want me to come to their church or their conference to speak. Most of the time I have to say no. I simply don't have time to be every place and still do my work as I should. They tell me that the Lord has led them to invite me. But it's strange the Lord would lead six different people to invite me for the same day! The Lord knows I can't be in six places at the same time.

If I were afraid of people and wanted simply to please people, I would find myself in the hospital. We must be very careful not to serve people but to serve God. If we are serving God as we should, we will find ourselves serving people too. There is always time to do the will of God. Paul said, "Ourselves your servants for Jesus' sake" (2 Cor. 4:5). He didn't say, "Ourselves your servants for *our* sake or for *your* sake." But he said, "For Jesus' sake."

Let me say a word to church members. Your pastor is not your slave. You say, "Well, if he doesn't do what I want him to do, I'll quit going to church." That's a very immature attitude to have. Your pastor is not there to be a slave to all the people. He is the servant of God. He may have to say no to you at times. When I was a pastor, folks would invite us over for meals or to one activity or another, and I would often have to say, "I'm sorry, we cannot come." Sometimes people would get disturbed. But I had work to do. I had meditating, praying, and writing to do. I had to live by my priorities.

We should not have to be enslaved to *the commandments of men*. In Matthew 15:9 the Lord Jesus warned us not to listen to the doctrines of men—the commandments of men. There is so much tradition these days! Churches have man-made traditions that cannot be backed up by the Word of God.

In John 5:41–44 Jesus warned about *the praise of men*. "I receive not honor from men. But I know you, that ye have not the love of God in you. . . . How can ye believe, who receive honor one of another, and seek not the honor that cometh from God only?" Beware of the praise of others. I fear that Christian workers often desire to please people and receive their praise and perhaps get a degree from some school or be used in an important meeting. This is dangerous.

In Galatians 1:10–12 Paul warned about *the authority of men*. My pastor has authority over me, and the government has authority over me. But Paul warned us not to allow people to dictate what our ministry should be and not to try to please people in our ministry. "For do I now seek the favor of men, or of God? Or do I seek to please men? For if I yet pleased men, I should not be the servant of Christ" (Gal. 1:10). That is a very plain statement! Some people bow down to please other people, bow to their authority; and by doing so, they are not serving God.

Beware of *the wisdom of men* (1 Cor. 2:5). Be sure you follow the wisdom of God. And beware of *the fear of men.* In Matthew 10:24–28, Jesus explained that all people can do is kill your body, but God can destroy both body and soul in hell!

Don't bow down to human commandments and traditions. Don't live for the praise of other people. Don't live under the dictatorial authority of people. Be careful that people are not running your life or your ministry. Watch out for the wisdom of people. Don't fear people. In other words, "Ye are bought with a price; be not ye the servants of men" (1 Cor. 7:23).

It is wonderful to discover this freedom from people, to not worry about whether they like you or dislike you, whether they approve or disapprove of your ministry. If you are doing the will of God, according to the Word of God, in the power of the Spirit of God, for the glory of God, then you are the servant of God. "Ye are bought with a price; be not ye the servants of men" (v. 23).

8

Freedom from the Past

e cannot change the past, but we can be changed by the past. Many people are controlled by past sins, past regrets, and past failures. The past should be a rudder to guide us and not an anchor to drag us back. In 1 Timothy 1:12–17 Paul wrote about his relationship to his past.

> And I thank Christ Jesus, our Lord, who hath enabled me, in that he counted me faithful, putting me into the ministry, who was before a blasphemer, and a persecutor, and injurious; but I obtained mercy, because I did it ignorantly in unbelief. And the grace of our Lord was exceedingly abundant with faith and love which is in Christ Jesus. This is a faithful saying, and worthy of all acceptance, that Christ Jesus came into the world to save sinners, of whom I am chief. Nevertheless, for this cause I obtained mercy, that in me first Jesus Christ might show forth all long-suffering, for a pattern to them who should hereafter believe on him to life everlasting. Now unto the King eternal, immor-

tal, invisible, the only wise God, be honor and glory forever and ever. Amen.

Paul was able to look at his past and, in spite of his failures, praise God. Paul was not shackled by past failures,
past sins, or past mistakes. You and I need to learn how to
be free from our past. Someone has said that most of the
people in the world are being crucified between two
thieves—the fear of tomorrow and the regrets of yesterday. How many people carry a heavy burden of past regret
and past failure! Though you cannot change the past, you
are being changed by the past. How can we be freed from
the tyranny of the past? I would suggest, on the basis of
Scripture, that we need to take some definite steps.

Accept God's Forgiveness

Paul said, "This is a faithful saying, and worthy of all
acceptance, that Christ Jesus came into the world to save
sinners, of whom I am chief" (1 Tim. 1:15). Paul had no
illusions about himself. He knew that what he had done
was wrong. He had been a blasphemer, and he had caused
other people to blaspheme. He had said, "Jesus Christ is
an imposter! He is not the Messiah!" He forced other people to make this confession. Paul was a persecutor. He was
injurious, or proud and insolent. A modern equivalent
would be our word "bully."

And yet Paul obtained mercy! He mentioned mercy in
verse 13 and again in verse 16. "Nevertheless, for this cause
I obtained mercy" (v. 16). In verse 14 he talked about "the
grace of our Lord." He also mentioned *faith* and *love* in
Christ Jesus. In other words, Paul eventually accepted
God's forgiveness. He confessed that he was a sinner. He
admitted that he had done wrong. He rested upon the
grace and the mercy of God. He experienced the love of

God and the abundance of the grace of God. God changed him!

If you are a Christian, God has completely dealt with all your sin—not just *part* of your sin but *all* of your sin. You are justified. That means God has declared you righteous in Jesus Christ, and that will never change. "Therefore, being justified by faith, we have peace with God" (Rom. 5:1). We can look at our past and know it's been taken care of. We can look at our present and know that God is with us. We can look at the future and know that God is going before us.

We have been regenerated. What does that mean? It means we have been born again. We have a new nature within us, and that new nature enables us to live a new life. We have been redeemed. We have been purchased out of the slavery of sin and set free to serve Jesus Christ. We are no longer slaves of sin, which means we are no longer slaves of the past. We have been forgiven—completely, totally, graciously—on the basis of Calvary. "In whom we have redemption through his blood, even the forgiveness of sins. . . . And you, being dead in your sins and the uncircumcision of your flesh, hath he made alive together with him, having forgiven you all trespasses" (Col. 1:14; 2:13).

I think it was Dr. Ironside who had this experience. He had been preaching on the fact that when you trust Jesus as your Savior, *all* of your sins are forgiven—past, present, and future. Someone approached him afterward and said, "I believe that when I was saved, Jesus took care of my *past* sins but not my future sins." Dr. Ironside quietly asked, "And how many of your sins were past when Jesus died?" That solves the problem, doesn't it?

Don't allow the fact that you used to be a wicked person before you trusted Jesus to cripple your life and ministry today. You are a new person in Jesus Christ. You still have all the potential for sin, but you have experienced the grace of God, the love of God, the mercy of God. Paul called himself the chief of sinners, and yet he accepted God's forgiveness. He believed in Jesus Christ, and this freed him from his past. We need to accept God's forgiveness.

An interesting story in Genesis 50 relates to Joseph and his brothers. You know, of course, that Joseph's brothers lied about him and sold him as a slave. Then Joseph became the second in command in Egypt. Joseph had the power and authority to prosecute his brothers, if he had wanted to; instead, he wept and forgave them. But they had a difficult time accepting his forgiveness! When their father, Jacob, died, the brothers were sure that Joseph would really "take it out on them." So they sent a messenger to Joseph and said, "Our father told us to be sure to tell you to forgive us." Joseph wept and said in effect, "Don't you believe me? I've already told you that I have forgiven you!"

Don't be shackled by the past. Live for the present. That is step one: Accept God's forgiveness.

Forgive Others

One evidence of true repentance is that we can forgive others. "If ye forgive men their trespasses, your heavenly Father will also forgive you; but if ye forgive not men their trespasses, neither will your Father forgive your trespasses" (Matt. 6:14–15). Our Lord was not saying that we have to *earn* forgiveness. He was saying that we have to give evidence of a broken heart. If I want to receive God's forgiveness, I have to repent of my sin and turn my back on it—and that includes an unforgiving spirit toward others.

In Matthew 18 the Lord Jesus told His disciples to forgive one another. Peter asked, "Well, if my brother sins against me, how many times should I forgive him? Seven times?" (see v. 21).

Jesus said, "Until, seventy times seven" (v. 22). That's 490 times! Obviously, my brother is not going to repeat the same sin 490 times. *But I may remember his sin 490 times!* I think our Lord was saying, "Every time you think about what your brother did to you, forgive him." Then He told the parable about the king who audited his books and discovered that one of his servants was robbing him of a large amount of money. So the king was going to sell the man and all that he had to pay the debt. But the man fell before the king and begged for forgiveness, and the king forgave him. But the servant went out of the king's presence and found a fellow servant who owed him just a few dollars. He grabbed the man, shook him and said, "Pay me what you owe me!" The man begged for forgiveness, but the servant ignored his request and threw the man in prison.

This servant was forgiven a huge debt, but he would not forgive his fellow servant a very small debt. That unforgiving servant was handed over to tormentors to be punished until he paid his debt. Sometimes God's people carry with them the shackles of the past because they have an unforgiving spirit. "And be ye kind one to another, tenderhearted, forgiving one another, even as God, for Christ's sake, hath forgiven you" (Eph. 4:32).

William Sangster was a great Methodist preacher in Great Britain. One Christmas he was making out his Christmas card list. His wife looked at the list and said, "Surely you're not going to send a card to *him*," naming the person. Sangster asked, "Why not?" His wife asked, "Do you remember what he did to you and what he said about you?" Sangster thought for a moment and said, "Oh yes, yes, now I do remember—but I had made it a point to remember to forget."

All of us need to remember to forget. We must learn to forgive others. That's step two.

Forgive Yourself

Many people cannot forgive themselves. Do you know why? Because they are proud. They say, "I told a lie, and I can't forgive myself!" Abraham lied about his wife. They say, "I lost my temper, and I was so angry!" Moses lost his temper one day and killed a man. He also lost his temper and disobeyed God by striking the rock. They say, "I've had such impure thoughts! How could I do that?" David had impure thoughts and committed some impure deeds. They say, "I denied the Lord! I could have stood up and witnessed, but I didn't!" Peter denied the Lord three times.

Are you better than any of these men? Pride makes me say, "Oh, how could I have done that?" But humility ought to make me say, "I'm surprised I don't do worse." You can't drive these thoughts out of your mind. You say, "I wish I could forget what I said to her." "I wish I could forget what I did to him," but you cannot. If you bury these thoughts in your personality, they will just create problems.

What should you do? *When you remember these thoughts, turn them into prayer and praise.* When you remember the things you have done, forgive yourself, and you will end up doing what Paul did—praising God: "Now unto the King eternal, immortal, invisible, the only wise God, be honor and glory forever and ever" (1 Tim. 1:17). God was able to use Paul as a pattern and as encouragement to others.

Forgive yourself. Don't hold grudges against yourself. Turn your memories of sin into praise and prayer. Trust God to bring something good out of it. You may not see how any good can come out of what you did, so leave it to God.

I have often reminded people that David committed two great sins: he committed adultery with Bathsheba (a sin of the flesh), and he numbered the people and took a census (a sin of the spirit). Seventy thousand people died because David numbered the people.

But the interesting thing is what God did with all this. David married Bathsheba, and Solomon was born. When David confessed his sin of numbering the people, he built an altar on a piece of property he had bought, and on that piece of property *Solomon built the temple.* Only God can take a man's two greatest sins and build a temple out of it.

You may have done some things that were wrong. You suffered the consequences of it, and you confessed it. God has forgiven you. Now, forgive yourself, and trust God to work out His purposes in your life. Only God can take a man's two greatest sins and build a temple out of them. I don't understand how God works all things together for good, but He does.

So we can see the three steps we need to take if we want to be set free from the past. First, *accept God's forgiveness.* Just believe the Word of God—that God has forgiven you of all your trespasses. He has cast your sins into the depths of the sea (see Micah 7:19). They are behind His back (see Isa. 38:17). They are remembered against you no more (see Heb. 10:17). As far as the east is from the west, He has removed your transgressions from you (see Ps. 103:12). Accept God's full and free forgiveness.

Second, *forgive others.* If you're harboring anything against anybody else, confess it to God, and confess it to them if necessary. It will set you free. The greatest freedom in the world is the freedom of forgiveness. This business of having family squabbles and misunderstandings so that you don't talk to people is foolish and sinful. Paul wrote to the Philippians: "Forgetting those things which are behind" (3:13). It is terrible to be living in the past when you ought to be living for the future. Forgive others.

Finally, *forgive yourself.* Quit being so proud. You're no better than any other person. God knows your frame; he remembers that you are dust (see Ps. 103:14). Don't try to drive the memories of sin out of your mind. Just turn them into praise and prayer. Just pray, "Lord, I know I shouldn't have said that. When I think about what I did, it bothers me. But I'm committing it to you now, and I'm going to praise you because I know you are going to bring something good out of it. Thank you for forgiving me." Turn those thoughts into praise and prayer as Paul did. Be a faithful servant of Jesus Christ, and trust the abundant grace of God to see you through.

Many people are being crucified between two thieves—the fears of tomorrow and the regrets of yesterday—and they cannot enjoy today. If you are in bondage to your past, turn it over to Jesus Christ. He is the God of your yesterdays, your todays, and your tomorrows, and He will set you free.

9

Freedom from Things

*L*et's think together about the problem of worry
and how to be set free from bondage to things.
I think this is one of the greatest needs Christians have today—to be delivered from things. We live in
a world saturated with things. How easy it is for us to get
attached to things and to be controlled by things.

Christians don't like to admit that they worry. They call
it being "burdened" or being "concerned," but worry is
what it really is. Jesus dealt with this problem in Matthew
6:19–34, a familiar passage.

> Lay not up for yourselves treasures upon earth, where moth
> and rust doth corrupt, and where thieves break through
> and steal, but lay up for yourselves treasures in heaven,
> where neither moth nor rust doth corrupt, and where
> thieves do not break through nor steal; for where your treasure is, there will your heart be also. The lamp of the body
> is the eye; if, therefore, thine eye be healthy, thy whole

body shall be full of light. But if thine eye be evil, thy whole body shall be full of darkness. If, therefore, the light that is in thee be darkness, how great is that darkness!

No man can serve two masters; for either he will hate the one, and love the other; or else he will hold to the one, and despise the other. Ye cannot serve God and money. Therefore, I say unto you, Be not anxious for your life, what ye shall eat, or what ye shall drink; nor yet for your body, what ye shall put on. Is not the life more than food and the body than raiment? Behold the fowls of the air; for they sow not, neither do they reap, nor gather into barns, yet your heavenly Father feedeth them. Are ye not much better than they? Which of you by being anxious can add one cubit unto his stature? And why are ye anxious for raiment? Consider the lilies of the field, how they grow; they toil not, neither do they spin, and yet I say unto you that even Solomon, in all his glory, was not arrayed like one of these. Wherefore, if God so clothe the grass of the field, which today is, and tomorrow is cast into the oven, shall he not much more clothe you, O ye of little faith? Therefore, be not anxious saying, What shall we eat? Or, What shall we drink? Or, With what shall we be clothed? For after all these things do the Gentiles seek. For your heavenly Father knoweth that ye have need of all these things. But seek ye first the kingdom of God, and his righteousness, and all these things shall be added unto you. Be, therefore, not anxious about tomorrow; for tomorrow will be anxious for the things of itself. Sufficient unto the day is its own evil.

The English word *worry* comes from an old Anglo-Saxon word that means "to strangle." The Greek word translated "being anxious" or "being troubled" in the Bible means "to be pulled apart." Worry is dangerous. It will strangle you physically, emotionally, and spiritually. It will pull you apart. It can create all kinds of problems, and the only person who can control it is the Christian himself. You and I must determine that things are not going to master our lives. One major cause of worry in our lives is our concern about things, our bondage to things. One of the evidences that we are getting all wrapped up in things is that we worry about them. If we want to have peace, we must learn how to be free from things. Jesus shared several truths with us that will help us to enjoy freedom from things.

It Is Not Wrong to Own Things

First of all, our Lord made it clear that *it is not wrong to own things.* In Genesis 1:31 we read: "And God saw every thing that he had made, and, behold, it was very good." It is not wrong to own things for several reasons.

God Made Things That Are Good

To begin with, *God made things.* In this universe there is God, there are people, and there are things. God is to be worshiped, people are to be loved and served, and things are to be used. God made things, and He did not make anything that is wrong. Things can be used in the wrong way, but they are not sinful in themselves. God made them.

Second, Genesis 1:31 states that *everything God made was good.* In fact, the verse tells us that it was *very* good. So God made things and things are good.

God Knows We Need Things

Third, *God knows that we need things.* "For your heavenly Father knoweth that ye have need of all these things" (Matt. 6:32). We don't need everything, but we do need basic things.

I was in a restaurant recently, waiting to be seated, and a young family came in. The father and mother and two little boys had to wait with the rest of us to be seated.

The younger of the two boys saw a candy machine that contained suckers. The little boy began to jump up and down and cry and hit his mother and say, "I want a sucker! I want a sucker!" Of course, his mother and father were very embarrassed because this is not the way little boys are supposed to act. (I was a little surprised they did not do something about it, but that's another sermon.) This little boy wanted *things,* and he was determined to get them even if he had to upset the entire restaurant and embarrass his mother and father.

Life is not measured by things. When a person dies, someone may ask, "How much did he leave?" He left *everything!* Life is not measured by things. "Take heed, and beware of covetousness; for a man's life consisteth not in the abundance of the things which he possesseth" (Luke 12:15). Mark Twain said, "Civilization is a limitless multiplication of unnecessary necessities." We get all wrapped up in things.

God Wants Us to Enjoy and Use Things

Fourth, *God wants us to enjoy things.* First Timothy 6:17 says, "Charge them that are rich in this age, that they be not highminded, nor trust in uncertain riches but in the living God, who giveth us richly all things to enjoy." God wants us to enjoy things. He made things. They are good, and it is not wrong to enjoy them.

Finally, *God wants us to use things.* In First Timothy 6:18 Paul said that we should do good, be rich in good works, be ready to distribute, and be willing to share. We should not only *enjoy* things, but we should *employ* things for the good of others and for the glory of God.

Here, then, are five reasons why it is not wrong to own things. God made things. Things are good. We need things. God wants us to enjoy things, and we can use things for the good of others and for the glory of God.

It Is Wrong for Things to Own Us

Our Lord gave us a second truth: *It is wrong for things to own us.* Things are marvelous servants but terrible masters. Matthew 6:21 says, "For where your treasure is, there will your heart be also." *Your heart* can start to love things. The word for this in the Bible is "covetousness." Covetousness means that we must have more things, bigger things, greater things. Then we start to measure life by things. It is possible for your heart to get wrapped up in things. When this happens, you start worrying because your heart gets divided. You get pulled apart.

It is possible for *the mind* to get all wrapped up in things. Matthew 6:22–23 says, "The lamp of the body is the eye; if, therefore, thine eye be healthy, thy whole body shall be full of light. But if thine eye be evil [defective], thy whole body shall be full of darkness. If, therefore, the light that is in thee be darkness, how great is that darkness!'

If your mind is fixed on things, then things will control you and the inner man will get darker and darker. Christ was talking here about conscience. Your conscience is like a window that lets the light into your inner man. As that window gets dirtier and dirtier, less light comes in, and then the light turns into darkness. If I allow my mind to get wrapped up in things, if my outlook is only on things, it will lead to inner darkness.

Things can control your *heart*. "Where your treasure is, there will your heart be also" (v. 21). Things can control your *mind*. Things can also control your *will*. "No man can serve two masters; for either he will hate the one, and love the other; or else he will hold to the one, and despise the other. Ye cannot serve God and money" (v. 24).

A divided life is a destroyed life. If you start living for things, things will become your master, and this will destroy your life. Worry is the evidence that the mind, the heart, and the will are possessed by things. That's why our Lord said in verse 25, "Therefore, I say unto you, Be not anxious for your life, what ye shall eat, or what ye shall drink; nor yet for your body, what ye shall put on. Is not the life more than food and the body than raiment?" Our Lord Jesus was saying, "When you start living for things and looking for things and loving things, your inner person starts to deteriorate, and the evidence of this is anxiety. Don't be anxious about your life." "Which of you by being anxious can add one cubit unto his stature?" (v. 27). You can't grow taller or live longer by worrying. Instead, worrying will shorten your life. "Therefore, be not anxious saying, What shall we eat? Or, What shall we drink? Or, With what shall we be clothed? For after all these things do the Gentiles [the lost] seek."

Worry is an evidence of unbelief. Unbelief is an evidence of disobedience. Disobedience is an evidence that something is wrong on the inside. What is wrong? Your heart, mind, and will are possessed by things. It is not wrong to own things, but it is wrong for things to own us.

Perhaps you've heard about the Quaker who was watching his wealthy neighbor move in. As you know the Quakers believe in simplicity of life. The Quaker watched as the movers carried in a great deal of furniture and all sorts of knickknacks and different furnishings. Finally, the Quaker called his neighbor over and said, "Neighbor, I would have a word with thee." The neighbor asked, "What is it?" The Quaker replied, "Neighbor, if ever thou dost think that thou dost need something, come to see me— and I will tell thee how to get along without it!" That is a good philosophy. It leads us to our third instruction.

76

God Must Be the Master

God must be the Master of everything in our lives. The secret is Matthew 6:33. "But seek ye first the kingdom of God, and his righteousness, and all these things shall be added unto you." In other words, take things out of the *center* of your life, and let God put things where they really belong. When things become your master, life becomes cheap. When things become your master, life is divided, life is defeated. But when Jesus Christ is your Master, then everything in your life finds its proper place, and you start putting the proper price tags on the "furniture" of life. I fear that some people are paying a great price for the cheap things that possess them. Think of the energy and time that is spent on all of the "things" that are so important to you. And yet you may be losing your children, your friends, perhaps even your husband or wife. There are people in hospitals today who would give everything they own to get their health back, and yet many of them are in the hospital because they are living for things. They are worrying, being pulled apart, being strangled by the incessant drive for things. God must be the Master of everything in our lives.

What does it mean to seek first the kingdom of God and His righteousness? It means that God is first in our lives. First thing in the morning, we turn to God in prayer and worship. We turn to Him in the Word. The first day of every week we are in church. The first thing in our lives—the most important thing—is to please Him. When God is first and we are worshiping Him and not things, then people and things fall into their proper place.

Not only do we seek God, but we submit to Him—to His rule and to His righteousness. We are saying, "My Lord and my God!" We are not running our own schedule; we are letting God run our schedule. It is marvelous when God liberates you from the tyranny of things! You can read the newspapers and see all the advertisements and not feel like you have to own all those things. When your neighbor has something that may be more expensive or more showy than what you have, it doesn't bother you at all. You are learning how to be content with what you have. Instead of complaining about what you *don't* have, you are rejoicing about what you *do* have.

All of this takes faith. You have to trust Him to meet your needs. "But seek ye first the kingdom of God, and his righteousness [his rule and his righteousness], and all these things shall be added unto you" (v. 33). This is God's promise. Not *half* of these things, not *some* of them, but "all these things shall be added unto you." David said, "I have been young, and now am old; yet have I not seen the righteous forsaken, nor his seed begging bread" (Ps. 37:25).

I want to warn you that worry can affect you mentally, physically, emotionally, and spiritually. It will make you upset and uptight. You will not be able to be the husband, the wife, the worker, the pastor, the son, the daughter you ought to be. Give the whole thing to the Lord! Say, "From now on, I'm going to put Jesus Christ first in my life and seek to please Him. I'm going to submit to God every day— to His rule and His righteousness. I'm going to live to please Him, and I'm going to trust His promise that He will supply all the things I need."

If you want to be free from things, you must understand and obey certain truths. First of all, it is not wrong to own things. Second, it is wrong for things to own us. Third, God must be the Master of everything. Jesus said we should learn to live a day at a time. "Be, therefore, not anxious about tomorrow; for tomorrow will be anxious for the things of itself. Sufficient unto the day is its own evil" (Matt. 6:34). Live a day at a time. A day at a time submit to God and seek God. A day at a time let God give you the things that you need. *Whatever He doesn't give you isn't worth having.* My prayer is that each of us will learn the real value of things in relation to the spiritual value of life. Don't put the wrong price tags on the things of life. God will supply all of your needs according to His riches in glory (Phil. 4:19), if you'll just seek Him first and submit to Him.

10

Future Freedom

s Christians, we enjoy freedom *now*, but our greatest experience of freedom will take place in the future when Jesus returns. The Bible calls this "the glorious liberty of the children of God." Romans 8:18–23 is the key passage:

> For I reckon that the sufferings of this present time are not worthy to be compared with the glory which shall be revealed in us. For the earnest expectation of the creation waiteth for the manifestation of the sons of God. For the creation was made subject to vanity, not willingly but by reason of him who hath subjected the same in hope. Because the creation itself also shall be delivered from the bondage of corruption into the glorious liberty of the children of God. For we know that the whole creation groaneth and travaileth in pain together until now. And not only they, but ourselves also, who have the first fruits of the Spirit, even we ourselves groan within ourselves,

waiting for the adoption, that is, the redemption of our
body.

Contrast between Suffering and Glory

The Apostle Paul presented in this passage a series of
contrasts between the present and the future. The first
contrast is in verse 18—*the contrast between suffering and
glory.* "I reckon that the sufferings of this present time are
not worthy to be compared with the glory which shall be
revealed in us." Creation was good. God looked on everything he had made and said it was very good. But today it
is a *groaning* creation. Suffering occurs everywhere. One
day it shall be a *glorious* creation. The pattern that God has
established in this world is first suffering and then glory.
We see it in nature. During the autumn and the winter
seasons, in many parts of the world, you can see the suffering and the groaning. But then glory follows in the
spring, the summer, and the harvest. This was true in the
life of our Lord Jesus Christ—first the suffering and then
the glory. In 1 Peter this theme is repeated over and over
again—first the suffering and then the glory. The disciples
wanted the glory without the suffering. The Devil will give
you the suffering without the glory. But the Christian life
means first the suffering, then the glory. God has established this pattern.

God's purpose for this world from the beginning was
that of glory. Then sin came in and brought suffering. In
Romans 5 Paul explained how the fall of the first man
brought sin, suffering, death, and condemnation into the
world. But we have in Jesus Christ the assurance of future
glory. Paul expressed this same truth in 2 Corinthians
4:16–18: "For which cause we faint not; but though our
outward man perish, yet the inward man is renewed day
by day. For our light affliction, which is but for a moment,

worketh for us a far more exceeding and eternal weight of glory, while we look not at the things which are seen, but at the things which are not seen; for the things which are seen are temporal, but the things which are not seen are eternal."

The outward man is perishing. We are growing older, and more and more decay is setting in. But the inward man is being renewed day by day. We are becoming more and more like Jesus Christ. Our affliction is light and only for a moment when compared with the eternity of the glory that lies before us when Jesus comes. Today we are experiencing suffering, but in that future liberty of the children of God, there will be glory.

Contrast between Expectation and Manifestation

In Romans 8:19 is a second contrast—*expectation and manifestation.* "For the earnest expectation of the creation waiteth for the manifestation of the sons of God." Another way of saying this is "For the anxious longing of the creation waits eagerly for the revealing of the sons of God." All of nature is eagerly anticipating the return of Jesus Christ. All of nature is on tiptoe, eagerly expecting his return. That's more than we can say for some Christians. Some Christians live day after day as though Jesus never died and as though He were never coming back again. But nature is waiting, expecting the coming of our Lord Jesus Christ. The picture here is that of eager expectation, a person straining, standing on tiptoe, looking for that future hope.

Contrasted to expectation is *manifestation.* All of creation is waiting for the sons of God to be manifested. The word translated "manifestation" in verse 19 is the same Greek word that is translated "revealed" in verse 18. It is the same word that is used in the name of the Book of the Revelation. A time will come when the sons of God are going to be revealed. Today the world cannot see what we really are. The glory that God has put within us and the glory that God has given to us have not been revealed. "Beloved, now are we the children of God, and it doth not yet appear what we shall be" (1 John 3:2). We do know that when Jesus Christ returns, we are going to enter into this wonderful glory, "the glorious liberty of the children of God" (Rom. 8:21).

In verse 17 Paul mentioned our inheritance. "If children, then heirs—heirs of God, and joint heirs with Christ—if so be that we suffer with him, that we may be also glorified together." Jesus Christ has already been glorified. We are in Christ; therefore, we have the assurance of future glory. We are joint-heirs—whatever He inherits, we inherit. Jesus prayed to His Father, "Father, I will that they also, whom thou hast given me, be with me where I am, that they may behold my glory, which thou hast given me" (John 17:24). Today is a time of expectation, but when Jesus returns, it will be *manifestation*. God is going to be glorified when His Church is without spot or wrinkle or blemish, when we have been transformed and share His eternal glory.

Contrast between Vanity and Hope

In Romans 8:20 we have a third contrast: *A contrast between vanity and hope.* "For the creation was made subject to vanity, not willingly by reason of him [God] who hath subjected the same in hope." The word "vanity" means "futility, aimlessness." In the Old Testament it is the name Abel. Adam and Eve named their son "Abel," which means "vanity." You find the words "vanity" and "vanities" 38 times in Ecclesiastes. "Vanity of vanities; all is vanity" (1:2). It's the word for "breath" and "vapor."

There seems to be no reason for what is going on in this world. If you read the newspapers and listen to the news, you say, "What in the world is going on?" It all seems so vain and so futile. But in contrast to the seeming vanity of this creation, we have a blessed hope in Jesus Christ. God has subjected creation to his control. He is working out His plan, and this plan involves hope. Hope in the Bible is not "hope so." It is not like the little boy or girl who is hoping to get a bicycle for Christmas. It is not similar to anything the world is hoping for. Rather, our hope is a certainty. It is the blessed assurance of the future, and this assurance controls the present. God has a plan for this world, and this plan will be carried out.

We have a living hope. "Blessed be the God and Father of our Lord Jesus Christ, who, according to his abundant mercy, hath begotten us again unto a living hope by the resurrection of Jesus Christ from the dead, to an inheritance incorruptible, and undefiled, and that fadeth not away, reserved in heaven for you" (1 Peter 1:3–4). Today the world is subjected to vanity, but when Jesus returns, we will experience the fulfillment of this blessed hope, "the glorious liberty of the children of God" (Rom. 8:21).

Contrast between Bondage and Liberty

In Romans 8:21 we have a fourth contrast: the contrast between *the bondage of corruption and the liberty of God's children.* "Because the creation itself also shall be delivered from the bondage of corruption into the glorious liberty of the children of God." Now we know why all of creation is waiting for Jesus to come back: Creation cannot be delivered until *we* are delivered! Creation cannot experience glory until *we* experience glory! This is why all creation is waiting for the Creator to return. This is why the Church is waiting for the Redeemer to return.

Creation is in bondage. Because of sin, creation is under subjugation (v. 21). Creation will be delivered. Delivered from what? From bondage. What kind of bondage? The bondage of corruption, the bondage of decay. The law of sin and death is operating in nature. There is death, and death leads to decay. Out of that decay comes soil, and from that soil comes life, and the cycle repeats itself: life, death, decay. Your body is subject to the law of sin and death. If we should die, our bodies will turn to dust. When Jesus returns, we shall receive a glorified body.

We cannot break this cycle of life and death. It seems as though every spring, creation is struggling to try to bring forth something new, something that will last. Then autumn comes, and what was brought forth does not last. It dies and decays. One day we shall go to heaven where there is no death, no decay, no corruption, no defilement. We are going to an inheritance that God has prepared for us.

Contrast between Groaning and Redemption

This leads to the final contrast: the contrast between *groaning and redemption* (Rom. 8:22–23). "For we know that the whole creation groaneth and travaileth in pain together until now" (v. 22). Creation is groaning, groaning in travail like a woman giving birth to a child. In the springtime creation travails to bring forth something new, and then it decays and dies, just as in previous years. "And not only they, but ourselves also, who have the first fruits of the Spirit, even we ourselves groan within ourselves" (v. 23). We don't groan just because of our arthritis, rheumatism, headaches, and troubles. Even unsaved people can groan because their bodies hurt! We are groaning within ourselves, *waiting for Jesus to come.* We are groaning for glory. All of creation is groaning for glory, and you and I as Christians should be groaning for glory.

We have "the first fruits of the Spirit" (v. 23). That means we have the down payment of glory in our hearts. We know we are going to heaven because the Holy Spirit lives in our hearts. God said, "Here is the down payment. The Holy Spirit is my earnest, my assurance to you that one day I'm going to take you to heaven and that you shall share in my glory." We will have glorified bodies, bodies like Christ's glorious body. We will no longer face death and decay or all the pain and suffering of this life. We will enjoy "the glorious liberty of the children of God" (v. 21).

Romans 8:30 affirms that we have *already* been glorified. "Moreover, whom he did predestinate, them he also called; and whom he called, them he also justified; and whom he justified, them he also glorified." It doesn't say He *will* glorify us but that He already *has* glorified us. Then what are we waiting for? We are waiting for the *manifestation of that glory.* We are waiting for our adoption, the redemption of our bodies. Our inner man has already been redeemed, but the body has not yet been redeemed. One of these days the body will be redeemed, and our salvation will be complete.

What does this say to us as Christians? For one thing, we know that suffering is not forever. Suffering will be forever for the unsaved. If you don't know Jesus as your Savior, be prepared to suffer forever. You ought to trust the Savior now and be delivered from the law of sin and death. "The sufferings of this present time are not worthy to be compared with the glory which shall be revealed in us" (v. 18).

People today hurt and weep. They have difficulties and trials of one kind or another. Let's do what all nature is doing: Let's lift up our hearts and eagerly anticipate the coming of Jesus!

All of the vanity of life will one day be replaced by the fulfillment of hope. The bondage of corruption will be replaced by the glorious liberty of the children of God. The groaning will be replaced by the adoption, the redemption of our bodies. What a wonderful day it will be when Jesus Christ returns and takes us to heaven and shares His eternal glory with us!

Part 2

Conscience

When you drive in certain mountainous areas, especially where there are long steep inclines, you will usually see signs warning you to check your vehicle's speed and shift into a lower gear. Occasionally you will also see an "escape lane" that leads off the main highway and into a level place of sand and gravel where a runaway vehicle can be slowed down and stopped. Vehicles out of control can do a lot of damage to property and even kill innocent people.

In the Christian life, freedom without conscience is like one of those vehicles out of control. The believer who doesn't balance liberty with responsibility is a dangerous driver on the road of life. In my pastoral ministry, I've had to counsel some of these "freedom drivers" and warn them that freedom is for the maturing Christian, not for the little children in the family. Every maturing believer must have that inner control called conscience in good working order or freedom will become license, and license often leads to tragedy.

On March 22, 1994, a Russian passenger jet crashed in Siberia, killing all seventy-five people on board. When the authorities transcribed the messages on the black box, they were stunned to learn that the captain's sixteen-year-old son and twelve-year-old daughter were playing with the controls! "Daddy, can I turn this?" the daughter asked. The son took the wheel but had trouble controlling the plane. The crew pulled the plane out of a spin, but it was too late. The plane was only 1,300 feet off the ground and the crash was inevitable.

The lesson here is obvious: It takes training and experience to fly a plane, and it takes training and experience—and together they spell "maturity"—to manage a successful life. A mature conscience, one that functions under the leading of the Holy Spirit, is absolutely essential for the enjoyment of true Christian freedom.

Billy Graham once said, "Most of us follow our conscience as we follow a wheelbarrow. We push it in front of us in the direction we want to go." A wheelbarrow can't do the damage of a runaway truck or a falling jet plane, *but it can get you off the main road and heading in the wrong direction.* The first step toward a ruined life is playing games with conscience.

So, let's learn what the right rules are and how we can enjoy true freedom in Jesus Christ because of a healthy conscience. The chapters that follow will help you better understand what conscience is and how it functions in the life of the maturing Christian believer.

"Conscience" in the New Testament

John 8:9
Acts 23:1; 24:16
Romans 2:15; 9:1; 13:5
1 Corinthians 8:7, 10, 12; 10:25, 27, 28, 29
2 Corinthians 1:12; 4:2; 5:11
1 Timothy 1:5, 19; 3:9; 4:2
2 Timothy 1:3
Titus 1:15
Hebrews 9:9, 14; 10:2, 22; 13:18
1 Peter 2:19; 3:16, 21

11

"A Principle Within"

"I want a principle within / Of watchful, godly fear."
When Charles Wesley wrote those words, he
was expressing a truth concerning conscience. The
German philosopher Immanuel Kant wrote: "Two things
fill the mind with ever-increasing wonder and awe . . . :
the starry heavens above me and the moral law within me."

Something within the heart of every person *approves*
when we do right and *accuses* when we do wrong, and that
something is conscience.

The word "conscience" is found 32 times in the New
Testament (King James Version) and was used 21 times
by the Apostle Paul. If we are going to be successful in our
Christian lives, we must understand what conscience is
and how it functions.

I want to discuss two topics related to conscience. First,
the *definition:* What is conscience? Second, the *description:*
How is conscience pictured in the Word of God? If we

understand what conscience is and how it functions, it can change our lives.

Definition of Conscience

You cannot escape conscience. You have to live with your conscience. You can argue with your conscience. You can defile your conscience. You can harden your conscience. But you will never get rid of your conscience. It may misfunction because you force it to misfunction, but it will always be there. Sad is the life where conscience does not work the way God wants it to work!

What is conscience? The word "conscience" in our English language comes from two Latin words. *Com* means "with" or "together," and *scio* means "I know." From the Latin, our English word "conscience" means "to know with" or "to know together." To know with what? To know with ourselves and to know within ourselves. Conscience is that inner knowledge that helps me to know myself.

The Greek word used in the New Testament, *syneidēsis,* means exactly the same thing. It comes from two Greek words, *syn* and *oida,* that mean "to know with."

In New Testament days the word "conscience" was not a strange word. It was used by the Greek people in their everyday conversation. It meant "the pain that you feel when you do wrong." That's a good definition, isn't it?

An American Indian who was a Christian said, "In my heart there is an arrowhead with three points to it. If I do wrong, the arrowhead turns, and it cuts me. If I do wrong too much, I wear out the points and it doesn't hurt me quite so much." But when the pain is gone, watch out!

Conscience is that inner faculty that indicates to us whether our actions are right or wrong, according to the standards within our hearts. Oswald Chambers gave a good definition of conscience: "The conscience is that innate faculty in a man's spirit that attaches itself to the highest that the man knows." Conscience is not the law; conscience bears witness to the law. Conscience is not the standard; conscience bears witness to the standard. In different parts of the world there are different standards.

Let me illustrate this. When the British took over India as part of their empire, they found some practices that simply had to be abolished. One of these practices was to burn the widow of a deceased man on the funeral pyre. The British issued a law abolishing this practice.

One of the religious leaders among the Indian people came to a British leader and said, "Our conscience tells us that the widow must be burned." And he responded, "And our conscience tells us that if you do it, we'll hang you!" That gives the difference, doesn't it?

Conscience can guide us aright if we have the right standard. Everyone has experienced this. If you cheat on an examination, tell a lie or do something you simply should not do, your conscience bothers you. Something down inside keeps reminding you that you should not have done that. That's conscience. Of course, some people have so abused their conscience that it doesn't bother them anymore; for these people we can only feel pity.

When Adam and Eve sinned against God, they hid. Do you know why? Their consciences were bothering them. They were afraid.

When David cut off part of Saul's skirt while Saul was asleep, David's heart smote him (see 1 Sam. 24:1–6). That's conscience. He knew that he should not have done this to the king of Israel. Even though Saul was not a godly man, he was the king. David could not respect the man, but he had to respect the office. His conscience bothered him when he treated the king that way.

Proverbs 28:1 says, "The wicked flee when no man pursueth." That's conscience. We read that Herod, when he heard about the miracles Jesus was doing, thought that

John the Baptist had come back to life again. His conscience was bothering him. "John, whom I have beheaded; he is raised from the dead" (Mark 6:16). That's conscience.

Two Descriptions of Conscience

Let's look at two beautiful descriptions of conscience in the Bible. The Apostle Paul gave us one of them in Romans 2:14–15, and the Lord Jesus gave us another in Matthew 6:22–23. Paul compared conscience to an inner witness, an inner judge.

Paul's Description

"For when the Gentiles, who have not the law, do by nature the things contained in the law, these, having not the law, are a law unto themselves; who show the work of the law written in their hearts, their conscience also bearing witness, and their thoughts the meanwhile accusing or else excusing one another" (Rom. 2:14–15).

The Gentiles were never given the Law. The Law was given to the Jews. But the Gentiles have the *work* of the Law written in their hearts. Notice that Paul did not say they have *the Law* written in their hearts. That doesn't happen until you're saved. When you're saved, then the Holy Spirit begins to write God's Law in your heart and you know right from wrong. But even unsaved people can know right from wrong because their conscience bears witness.

In the inner man is a courtroom. A judge sits at the bench, and that judge is also the witness and the jury! That whole "group" in the courtroom is known as conscience. The judge does not make the law, he applies the law. When you and I do something right, then our conscience says, "That's good! That's good!" It does not accuse, it approves.

94

When we do something wrong, that inner judge, that inner witness, says to us, "You are wrong! You are wrong!" And it hurts.

Conscience, you see, is judicial. Conscience does not *pass* the law. Conscience does not *make* the law. Conscience *bears witness* to the law.

You and I can remember when we were little children, even before we understood all that was involved in ethics and morals, that when we did something wrong, something would bother us down inside. That was conscience.

Paul told us that conscience is an inner witness that indicates whether we have done right or wrong. "Their thoughts the meanwhile accusing or else excusing one another" (v. 15). Paul told us that *everyone* had this faculty. This is not something we have to develop. It is there. God has given every person a conscience.

Let me remind you once again, conscience is not the law. Conscience functions according to the law that we have. If we are given a standard and if that standard is not right, conscience will still work according to that standard. The important thing is to have the *right* standard so that our conscience can work the way God wants it to work.

Jesus' Description

This leads us to what our Lord Jesus said in Matthew 6:22–23: "The lamp of the body is the eye; if, therefore, thine eye be healthy, thy whole body shall be full of light. But if thine eye be evil, thy whole body shall be full of darkness. If, therefore, the light that is in thee be darkness, how great is that darkness!"

Paul compared conscience to a witness; Jesus compared conscience to a window. The window does not manufacture the light—the window lets the light in. You and I have this inner window through which God wants to shine His light. If that window gets dirty, less light can come in. Imagine the judge sitting in the courtroom at his desk. On this desk is the Law of God. Through the window comes the light, and that light shines upon the Law. Now, as that window gets dirtier, less light shines upon that Law, and that Law is less visible. If the window gets completely covered with dirt, it's impossible to see the Law. This is how conscience functions. That's why we say conscience witnesses to the highest standard we have. The highest standard, of course, is the Word of God.

Jesus said conscience is like your eye. The eye does not manufacture light—the eye lets light in. When the light comes into our lives, it gives us guidance. But suppose that every time we do something wrong, the window gets dirtier until finally we have sinned so much that the window is completely covered with dirt. The light cannot come through, and so we are left in the darkness!

It's a terrible thing when light turns into darkness. Our Lord did not say that the light disappears but that *the light turns into darkness!* What should lead us in the right path leads us in the wrong path. The Bible calls this an evil conscience.

Some people, if they do good, are bothered by it; but if they do evil, they are happy. That is an evil conscience. There are those who call evil "good" and good "evil." That's an evil conscience. Your conscience is like a window, and the window lets in the light. Don't let the light become darkness!

When a person becomes a Christian, God cleanses the conscience. No matter what we have done, no matter how we have sinned, God cleanses our conscience. And when the conscience is cleaned, then the light of God's Word can penetrate to our inner being. As we read the Word of God we discover that God has certain standards. Some things are right, and some things are wrong. We must not do or say or be involved in some things. As we obey God's Word, then the window gets cleaner and cleaner, and more light shines in.

Have you ever wondered why some Christians have more discernment than others? Have you ever wondered why some saints of God always seem to know where they're supposed to go and what they're supposed to do? They seem to have an inner compass that directs them. This is their conscience. The Holy Spirit wants to work with your conscience to guide you and to help you grow in the Christian life. This is why conscience is such a wonderful blessing, because a good conscience can help you live a good Christian life.

We're going to discover that there are many different kinds of conscience. Some people have a weak conscience. Some have a strong conscience. Some have a defiled conscience. Some have an evil conscience. You may be saying right now, "My conscience is really in trouble. It doesn't bother me anymore. I'm doing things today that, if I had done them a year ago, would have bothered me all night! But I don't worry anymore." This is not good, but God can cleanse your conscience.

Suppose that every time you sinned, you lost a little bit of your vision. How much sinning would you do? You say, "Oh, I wouldn't do much sinning! I wouldn't want to lose my sight!" That's true. But we do this to our conscience all the time.

Your conscience is a marvelous servant. It was designed to work for you and with you. When a person works toward having a good conscience, he becomes a good Christian, has a good witness for the Lord Jesus Christ and enjoys the good blessings God has for him. He never has to vacillate from one thing to another, asking, "Do I go here? Do I go there? What does God want me to do?" It's a beautiful experience to have a healthy conscience.

If something is wrong right now with your conscience, confess it to the Lord. Make it right with Him. Don't begin the day or the activities of life with a conscience that's defiled. The Lord Jesus Christ can forgive you and cleanse you and give you a healthy conscience. Then you can learn how to exercise that conscience and live to the glory of God.

12

God's Gift to You

*Y*our conscience is important, and you should be very careful what you do to it and with it. Let me give you eight reasons why your conscience is important.

Conscience Is God's Gift

Your conscience is important because *it is God's gift* to you. You were made "in the image of God" (Gen. 1:27). Being made in God's image means we have a mind to think with, a heart to feel with, and a will to decide with. Our basic nature is spiritual. A person is not just a body; he is fundamentally spiritual. Saint Augustine said, "Thou hast made us for Thyself, and the heart of man is restless until it finds its rest in Thee." One aspect of this image of God in people is the ability to distinguish right from wrong. Romans 2:14–15 tells us that people have a conscience. It's God's gift to them.

Scientists are trying to discover where conscience comes from. A number of false views about the origin of conscience have developed. Some say that conscience comes *from behind us*—it's a part of evolution. As man evolved over the centuries, conscience evolved with him. And yet Darwin in his book *The Descent of Man* said this: "Of all the differences between man and the lower animals, the moral sense, or conscience, is by far the most important." Even Darwin couldn't explain where conscience came from.

Conscience is not the by-product of evolution; it did not come from behind us. Nor did conscience come *from around us.* I hear people saying that conscience is merely the total of all the standards of the society around you.

The philosopher Schopenhauer said that conscience consisted of "one-fifth the fear of man, one-fifth superstition, one-fifth prejudice, one-fifth vanity and one-fifth custom." In other words, your conscience is a sort of "tossed salad" that you put together from the society around you.

Society does help to give us standards, but society does not give us the conscience. We have learned that conscience is that faculty *that responds to the standards we have.* Conscience does not manufacture the standards, and the standards do not manufacture the conscience. Conscience is the window that lets in the light—it doesn't manufacture the light. While people have different customs and standards in different parts of the world, conscience still functions the same way no matter where you go.

Conscience does not come from behind us, and conscience does not come from around us. Nor does conscience come *from within us.* Many psychiatrists want us to believe that we have manufactured our own conscience—it's the by-product of the way Mother raised us and the way Father disciplined us. I disagree with all these explanations. I think that conscience is the gift of God. According to the Word of God, conscience came *from above us.* Conscience is a universal phenomenon. Conscience is found everywhere in the world; therefore, it must have a common source, and that common source is God. God has put within the hearts of people this wonderful faculty called conscience. Therefore, you must be careful how you treat your conscience because it is God's gift to you.

Conscience Guides Our Conduct

There's a second reason why conscience is important: *Conscience guides our conduct.* I've heard people say, "Let your conscience be your guide," and to some degree this is good advice. It's important, however, for conscience to have the right guide, the right standard to follow.

In Acts 24:16 we read the words of the Apostle Paul: "In this do I exercise myself, to have always a conscience void of offense toward God, and toward men." Paul admitted that his conscience needed *exercise*. If conscience is not exercised, it will begin to function in the wrong way. It will no longer be "void of offense toward God, and toward men." But when conscience is functioning properly, it can guide us.

The Holy Spirit wants to use your conscience. In Romans 9:1 Paul wrote that *his conscience was bearing witness* in the Spirit of God. The Holy Spirit uses the Word of God to show us the will of God, and our conscience is involved in this process. If your conscience is functioning the way it should, then you have a compass to direct you, a light to guide you, and a law to give you wisdom in the Christian life.

Conscience Strengthens for Service

Conscience is important because it is God's gift to you and because it can guide your conduct. Third, conscience is important because *it strengthens you for Christian service.*

We read in 1 Timothy 1:5: "Now the end of the commandment is love out of a pure heart, and of a good conscience, and of faith unfeigned [sincere faith, not hypocritical faith]." The purpose of the ministry of the Word of God is that I might have love from a pure heart, that I might have a good conscience, and that I might have sincere faith that is not hypocritical.

First Timothy 1:19 says, "Holding faith, and a good conscience, which some, having put away concerning faith, have made shipwreck." When you start playing around with your conscience, you're heading for shipwreck. Conscience is the compass that guides us. When you don't follow that compass or when you try to change the compass, you're going to end up shipwrecked.

In 1 Timothy 3:9 Paul wrote that the deacons should hold "the mystery of the faith in a pure conscience." So conscience is connected very definitely to our ministry and our service as Christians.

In 2 Corinthians 4:2 Paul wrote: "But [we] have renounced the hidden things of dishonesty, not walking in craftiness, nor handling the Word of God deceitfully, but by manifestation of the truth commending ourselves to every man's conscience in the sight of God."

Second Corinthians 5:11 says, "Knowing, therefore, the terror of the Lord, we persuade men; but we are made manifest unto God, and I trust also are made manifest in your consciences."

In his ministry Paul was very careful to have a clear conscience and to minister to the consciences of others. Conscience is important because it strengthens us for Christian service. When your conscience is clear, you can face any enemy.

Conscience Strengthens Fellowship

Conscience also *strengthens our Christian fellowship.* We're going to discover from Romans 14 and 15 and from 1 Corinthians 8, 9, and 10 that some people have a strong conscience and some people have a weak conscience. Those with a weak conscience often create problems in the fellowship. Sometimes those who have a strong conscience do too, but usually it's the other way around.

Some in the Roman assemblies had a weak conscience, and they would not eat meat. Some in the Corinthian church had a strong conscience; they not only ate meat, but they also ate it at the idol temples and participated in idolatrous feasts. Paul wrote to those people and explained what it meant to have a weak conscience and what it meant to have a strong conscience.

You want to become the kind of Christian who has a strong conscience. A strong conscience does not give you the privilege of sinning! The person with a strong conscience claims the privileges and the freedoms that we have in the Word of God, enjoys these privileges and these freedoms, but never uses them to hurt others. We would solve a great many problems in our churches if we'd learn how to have a strong conscience. People are divided over everything under the sun. We Christians don't have enough faith to accept the truth of the Word of God and act upon it. Sometimes strong Christians don't know how to accept weak Christians and help them grow up in the Lord. Conscience strengthens our fellowship.

Conscience Encourages Witnessing

There is a fifth reason why your conscience is important: *It encourages your witness.* When you have a strong conscience and a good conscience, you aren't afraid to face the problems and difficulties of life. You see them as opportunities for witnessing.

First Peter 2:19 says, "For this is thankworthy, if a man for conscience toward God endure grief, suffering wrongfully." Anybody can suffer when he's done something wrong—that doesn't take much grace. But when you've done something *right* and you suffer for it, that's something else. What takes you through that suffering? A good conscience. When your conscience is right between you and God, it makes little difference what people say about you or do to you.

First Peter 3:15–16 says, "But sanctify the Lord God in your hearts, and be ready always to give an answer to every man that asketh you a reason of the hope that is in you, with meekness and fear, having a good conscience, that, whereas they speak evil of you, as of evildoers, they may be ashamed that falsely accuse your good manner of life [behavior] in Christ."

A good conscience encourages your witness. Nothing will shut your mouth like a conscience that convicts you. When we know we've done something wrong, when there's something between us and the Lord, we're not very good witnesses, are we?

Conscience Helps in Prayer

There's a sixth reason why we should have a good conscience: *It helps us in prayer.* First John 3:19–22 says, "And by this we know that we are of the truth, and shall assure our hearts before him. For if our heart condemn us, God is greater than our heart, and knoweth all things. Beloved, if our heart condemn us not, then have we confidence toward God. And whatever we ask, we receive of him, because we keep his commandments, and do those things that are pleasing in his sight."

If when I kneel to pray, my conscience convicts me, I have to get it straightened out before I can talk to God. If

I come to the Lord in prayer, and something is wrong in my life, my conscience will tell me about it. It's wonderful to be able to pray in the will of God and not be accused by our conscience.

The psalmist said, "If I regard iniquity in my heart, the Lord will not hear me" (Ps. 66:18). Conscience helps us in our praying. As we face the Lord, if we have a good conscience, a conscience void of offense toward God and toward others, then we can pray effectively.

Jesus talked about this in the Sermon on the Mount. He said, "If you're going to the altar to offer your sacrifice and remember that there's something between you and your brother, leave your sacrifice. First go and be reconciled with your brother. Then come and offer your sacrifice" (see Matt. 5:23–24).

Conscience Affects Citizenship

There's a seventh reason why we should pay attention to our conscience and be careful how we treat it: *It affects our citizenship.*

Are there times when Christians should not obey the government? In Romans 13 we're told that every person should be subject to the higher powers because those higher powers are ordained of God. So we should obey the law because God has established government. We should obey the law because government has established punishment. If we don't obey, we'll be punished.

But in Romans 13:5 Paul said, "Wherefore, ye must needs be subject, not only for wrath but also for conscience sake." What is a conscientious objector? Is there such a thing in the Word of God as civil disobedience? If your conscience is functioning as it should, it helps you know when to obey and when not to obey the law.

105

Suppose you are told not to witness. Suppose, like Daniel, you are told not to pray. Suppose, like those Hebrew midwives, you are told to murder babies. What will you do? Conscience helps us in our citizenship. It helps us to be good citizens and to use our citizenship to the glory of God.

Conscience Helps Build Character

The eighth reason why we should care for our conscience is this: *It helps us to build character.* Hebrews 5:13–14 says, "For everyone that useth milk is unskillful in the word of righteousness; for he is a babe. But solid food belongeth to them that are of full age, even those who by reason of use have their senses exercised to discern both good and evil." The writer was talking here about growing and maturing in the Christian life. If you do not use your faculties, they could become useless. If a person ties his right arm to his body and doesn't use it, it will atrophy.

Our spiritual senses function in a similar way. If we don't exercise our spiritual senses, then we never learn how to discern between good and evil, and then we don't grow in Christian character. It is important for us to build up our conscience—to have a good conscience, a pure conscience, a conscience void of offense—because this helps us to build Christian character.

I trust I have convinced you from these eight reasons that your conscience is important. We cannot afford to fool around with, or toy with, conscience. Conscience is God's gift to you. It can guide your conduct, strengthen you for service, strengthen you in Christian fellowship, encourage you in your witnessing, help you in your praying, give you guidance concerning your citizenship, and ultimately help you to build your character. This is why Charles Wesley wrote in that hymn: "I want a principle within / Of watch-ful, godly fear." That principle is conscience.

If you don't know Jesus Christ personally, trust Him as your Savior. He will cleanse your conscience, and then it will help build your life to the glory of God.

13

A Good Conscience

Conscience is one of the servants God has given us to help us in our Christian life. The New Testament speaks of many different kinds of conscience: a *pure* conscience as well as a *defiled* conscience, a *good* conscience and an *evil* conscience, a *strong* conscience and a *weak* conscience.

We want to focus on the characteristics of a good conscience. The Apostle Paul said in Acts 24:16, "And in this do I exercise myself, to have always a conscience void of offense toward God, and toward men."

What are the characteristics of a good conscience? It has at least three characteristics.

A Good Conscience Is Effective

First, *a good conscience is effective*. It works. If you had an automobile that didn't run, you wouldn't call it a good automobile. You'd just call it an automobile that's not running. If you have a conscience that is not operating effectively, you could not call it a good conscience. A good conscience is one that actually works in our lives.

Keeps Us on Course

A good conscience effectively keeps us on course. "As I besought thee to abide still at Ephesus, when I went into Macedonia, that thou mightest charge some that they teach no other doctrine, neither give heed to fables and endless genealogies, which minister questions rather than godly edifying which is in faith, so do. Now the end [object] of the commandment is love out of a pure heart, and of a good conscience, and of faith unfeigned, from which some, having swerved, have turned aside unto vain jangling" (1 Tim. 1:3–6).

Paul warned Timothy to stick to the doctrines of the Word of God. They help us develop a good conscience, and a good conscience will keep us on course.

Verse 6 uses the phrase "have turned aside." This phrase means they have missed the mark, they have swerved, they have gone off course. You see, God has a course for each of us, and we had better stay on that course. If we don't stay on course, we won't achieve the purposes God has for us. A good conscience keeps us from going off course to fables and foolish arguments.

In my ministry of more than fifty years now, I have seen many people go off course in their Christian walk. They simply have not been on target. They've gotten off on some detour, some trivial thing. Some of them, unfortunately, have gotten off into sin and unbelief. A good conscience will keep you from doing this.

Helps Us Be Victorious

Second, *a good conscience will help you to have victory.* First Timothy 1:18–19 says, "This charge I commit unto thee, son Timothy, according to the prophecies which pointed to thee, that thou by them mightest war a good warfare, holding faith, and a good conscience, which some, having put away concerning faith, have made shipwreck."

First you go off course, and then you wreck the ship. We are in a battle. We must fight a good warfare. Some warfare is bad, but this is a good warfare, a warfare against the world, the flesh, and the Devil. Those who have faith and a good conscience can fight the battle and win the victory. Nothing gives you greater courage as you face the battles of life than a good conscience, one that is functioning well in your life.

Timothy had some battles in Ephesus where he pastored. That would not be an easy place to pastor. Ministers write to me or phone me and say, "Brother Wiersbe, I am in a rough place!" There are no easy places. Wherever you lift the banner of Jesus Christ, the Devil is going to fight you, and if he can, he will use the members of the church to do it! If you hold onto faith and a good conscience, you can wage the good warfare.

Helps Us Be Honest

A good conscience not only keeps us on course and helps us to have victory, but *a good conscience will also help us to be honest.* Hebrews 13:18 says, "Pray for us; for we trust we have a good conscience, in all things willing to live honestly." The word translated "honestly" means "beautifully, seemingly, fittingly." The Christian life is to be a beautiful life. Christians should not create problems—they should solve problems. Usually a Christian doesn't create problems, he reveals them. The problems were already there. But if you have a good conscience, you will be able to live an honest life, a beautiful life. People will look at you and say, "There is something about him or her that is really lovely."

It's unfortunate when Christians don't pay their bills. It's unfortunate when Christians have a bad reputation in the business community. If a person has a good conscience, he will live honestly, pay his bills, and keep his promises. He will be true to his contracts because his conscience will help him to live honestly.

Keeps Us Witnessing

In 1 Peter 3:14–17 we discover that *a good conscience is effective to keep us witnessing.* "But and if ye suffer for righteousness' sake, happy are ye: and be not afraid of their terror, neither be troubled, but sanctify the Lord God in your hearts, and be ready always to give an answer to every man that asketh you a reason of the hope that is in you, with meekness and fear, having a good conscience, that, whereas they speak evil of you, as of evildoers, they may be ashamed that falsely accuse your good manner of life [behavior] in Christ. For it is better, if the will of God be so, that ye suffer for well-doing than for evil-doing."

Peter was writing to people who were being falsely accused. That's a hard thing to experience. They were being accused of saying and doing things that they had not said and done. How were they to prove that these accusations were wrong? Were they supposed to go to court? Were they supposed to hold a protest meeting? No, he simply said, "Be ready to witness."

Obstacles can become opportunities. When people are making trouble for you, it is an opportunity to witness if you have a good conscience. If you've done evil, your conscience will rebuke you and convict you, but if you are doing good, your conscience will strengthen you. There is nothing like a good conscience to keep you strong when people are lying about you.

A good conscience is an effective conscience. It keeps us on course, keeps us victorious, keeps us honest and keep us witnessing when the going is tough. The person who abandons a good conscience begins to swerve off course and to move toward the dangerous reefs of life, and before long he is shipwrecked.

This is what happened to King Saul. King Saul began to play with his conscience, and before long he got off course. Then he lost the victory and began to lie and make excuses. Before long he was dead. It is an important thing to have a good conscience. A good conscience is effective.

A Good Conscience Is Enlightened

The second characteristic of a good conscience is this: *A good conscience is enlightened. A* good conscience is taught by the Word of God and guided by the Spirit of God.

The Lord Jesus compared conscience to a window that lets in light. Matthew 6:22–23 says, "The lamp of the body is the eye; if, therefore, thine eye be healthy, thy whole body shall be full of light. But if thine eye be evil, thy whole body shall be full of darkness. If, therefore, the light that is in thee be darkness, how great is that darkness!"

Conscience is a window that lets in the light, and the more light you have from the Word of God, the better our conscience is going to function. Conscience attaches itself to the highest standard that the person knows. As we grow in our Christian life, our standard gets higher and higher.

When we first meet the Lord, we have many things to learn. As the light begins to shine into our hearts, we see the cobwebs and the dust, and we begin to clean things up. The more knowledge you have about God and the more knowledge you have about the grace of God, the better your conscience will function. This is why we must read the Word of God, exhort one another, and seek the light from the Holy Spirit.

In 1 Corinthians 8 Paul made it clear that *knowledge* and *conscience* go together. The consciences of some people don't bother them because they don't have the knowledge that should enlighten their consciences. Some people do not have any light; they have darkness—the darkness of superstition and ignorance.

When John Knox was preaching the Gospel in Scotland and seeking to reform the church, Queen Mary, who had a different belief, opposed him. She said to him one day, "My conscience is not so." John Knox replied to Queen Mary, "Conscience, Madam, requires knowledge, and I fear that right knowledge you have none."

A Good Conscience Is Exercised

A good conscience is effective. A good conscience is enlightened. And third, *a good conscience is exercised.*

Paul told Felix, "And in this do I exercise myself, to have always a conscience void of offense toward God, and toward men" (Acts 24:16). Our conscience, like our muscles, must be exercised. If our conscience lies dormant and is not exercised, then it becomes an evil conscience.

Hebrews 5:13–14 describes this: "For everyone that useth milk is unskillful in the word of righteousness; for he is a babe. But solid food belongeth to them that are of full age, even those who by reason of use have their senses exercised to discern both good and evil."

113

Each of our physical senses can be exercised to an amazing degree of proficiency. People can be taught to hear better or to see clearer. Some people have an amazing sense of touch. Even the sense of taste can be trained to a marvelous degree of proficiency. In the same way our spiritual senses—our spiritual sight, our spiritual hearing, our spiritual taste—must be exercised if we're going to have discernment, and this involves conscience.

Conscience must be exercised, otherwise it cannot be a good conscience. And you exercise your conscience when you obey the Word of God, when you do the things God tells you to do. Just as a musician develops skill as he practices his music, just as a cook develops skill as she continually prepares meals, or an artist develops skill the more he paints—so the Christian develops a keen sensitivity about what is right and wrong as he obeys the Word of God. A good conscience is one that is exercised.

The Greek word *apeiros* translated "unskillful" in Hebrews 5:13 means "without experience." The Greek word *gymnazō* translated "exercise" in verse 14 gives us our English word *gymnasium*. The Greeks were great believers in physical exercise. The writer of Hebrews is saying, "Just as you exercise your physical senses and your physical muscles, so you must exercise your spiritual senses and your conscience, for a good conscience is one that is exercised."

Do you have a good conscience? Is your conscience effective? Is it working? When you have done something wrong, does your conscience bother you? When you do something right and people oppose you, does your conscience strengthen you?

I trust that your conscience is an enlightened conscience and that you are growing in your knowledge of the Word of God. I trust you aren't living by custom or tradition but by the truth of the Word of God.

It is thrilling when you are not only *walking* in the light of God's Word but also *carrying* the light with you wherever you go.

Do you have an exercised conscience? Or do you say, "Well, what difference does it make?" The only way to grow as a Christian, the only way to stand as a Christian, the only way to be effective as a Christian is to exercise your conscience and to grow toward maturity in the Lord. It's a wonderful thing to have a good conscience. Do everything you can to keep your conscience in good repair. Once a good conscience starts to fail, you're moving toward shipwreck.

May the Lord help us to have a good conscience.

14

A Weak Conscience

The Apostle Paul devoted nearly five chapters in two of his letters to the problems caused by people who have a weak conscience: 1 Corinthians 8, 9, and 10 and Romans 14 and 15. God wants us to develop a strong conscience because Christians who have a weak conscience can create problems for themselves and for other believers. In fact, I am convinced that many of the divisions and dissensions in churches today and across the evangelical world are caused by people who have a weak conscience.

Let's consider this matter of a weak conscience by looking at three important topics.

Characteristics of a Weak Conscience

First, let's consider *the characteristics of a weak conscience.* How can I tell whether or not I am a Christian with a weak conscience? There are at least eight characteristics of the person with the weak conscience.

Saved and in the Church

First of all, he *is* saved. Let's make this very clear. He is saved, and second he is in the church. In Romans 14:1 Paul said, "Him that is weak in the faith receive ye, but not to doubtful disputations." In other words, this person is a Christian, and he is in the church. He's not supposed to be kept out of the church because he has a weak conscience.

Lacks Knowledge

Third, he lacks knowledge. In 1 Corinthians 8:7 we read these words: "However, there is not in every man that knowledge; for some with conscience of the idol unto this hour eat it [this food] as a thing offered unto an idol, and their conscience, being weak, is defiled."

The problem in the Corinthian church was "Should a Christian eat meat that's been offered on the altar of some idol?" The cheapest meat in Corinth was available from the butcher shops at the temples. The strong Christians said, "An idol is nothing, and meat offered to an idol is not defiled; so I'll buy that meat." The weak Christians said, "Oh, no! We were saved out of idolatry, and that meat has been defiled!" and so the weak Christians did not have enough knowledge to understand spiritual things. They were still living, as it were, in infancy, and they didn't realize that food itself is neither good nor bad in relation to the spiritual life.

Easily Wounded and Offended

A fourth characteristic is that the person with the weak conscience is easily wounded and offended. First Corinthians 8:12 says, "but when ye sin so against the brethren, and wound their weak conscience, ye sin against Christ." Romans 14:15 says, "But if thy brother be grieved with thy food, now walkest thou not in love. Destroy not him with thy food, for whom Christ died."

Unstable

The person with the weak conscience is very easily wounded, very easily offended, and he's bothered by the freedom practiced by those who have a strong conscience. This leads to the fifth characteristic: He's very unstable, and he stumbles very easily. Romans 14:13 says, "Let us not, therefore, judge one another any more; but judge this, rather: that no man put a stumbling block or an occasion to fall in his brother's way."

Little children who are immature stumble over the smallest things. But adults, who have learned how to walk and balance themselves, are not usually troubled by those things.

Critical of Others

A sixth characteristic of a person with a weak conscience is this: He is very critical of others. Romans 14:3–4 says, "Let not him that eateth despise him that eateth not; and let not him who eateth not judge him that eateth; for God hath received him. Who are thou that judgest another man's servant? To his own master he standeth or falleth. Yea, he shall be held up; for God is able to make him stand."

In the Roman church the problem was what you should eat and on what day you should honor God. They had problems with diets and days. The weaker Christians said, "Oh, we cannot eat this meat! We cannot eat these things!" The stronger Christians said, "You can eat anything." The weak Christians said, "Certain days are very special, and we must commemorate these days." The stronger Christians said, "Every day is a good day if you're walking with the Lord." The result was a divided church because the weaker Christians were critical of the stronger Christians.

Legalistic

The Christian with the weak conscience is legalistic. He lives by rules and regulations because he fears freedom. He is like a child. A child enjoys being smothered by Mother's love—he enjoys the protection. Then one day Mother says, "OK, you're going off to school." The child says, "I don't want to go to school." So he runs home from school, or he hides when he should be going to school. Why? He's afraid of freedom. It's dangerous to cross the street; it's dangerous to be thrown into a crowd of people you don't know. Mature adults don't worry about that. In fact, as we mature in the Lord we are happy to have new experiences, to meet new people, to face new challenges.

The person with the weak conscience is legalistic. He follows many rules and regulations. Please understand, I am not opposing standards. Mature adults must have standards. There are some things we will not do because we know better. But that's not what we build our lives on. We have standards because we love the Lord, because we love one another, because we've learned to appreciate the things that are good and holy and right. But the person with the weak conscience is very legalistic. He measures everybody else by his rules, and he is very easily offended if you do something different from the way he does it.

Confused Priorities

Finally, the person with the weak conscience has his priorities confused. He focuses on the externals and not on the internals and the eternals. Romans 14:17 says, "For the kingdom of God is not food and drink, but righteousness, and peace, and joy in the Holy Spirit." The weak saints have a list of rules and regulations concerning what to eat and what not to eat, where to go and where not to go. But Paul said that these external things are not the important things. They are the by-products of what God is doing in your heart. Therefore, don't get your priorities confused.

Some people have the idea that the person with the rigid rules and regulations is the one with the strong conscience, and the person who exercises freedom in the Lord has the weak conscience. But it's just the other way around! The person with the strong conscience is tolerant of the differences he sees in other people. The person with the strong conscience does not stumble or become easily offended because of what somebody says or does. The person with the weak conscience is the person who, when he sees one thing in a magazine that he doesn't like, cancels his subscription. The Christian with the weak conscience is the one who, when he hears a piece of music he doesn't like, either leaves the church or stops supporting the radio ministry. The person with the weak conscience is the one who, when the preacher uses a different translation from what he prefers, will not support that church any more. That person is not spiritual at all; he has a lot of growing to do.

The Cause of a Weak Conscience

This leads to our second topic: *What is the cause of a weak conscience?* Why are people in our churches easily offended, critical, unstable, and legalistic? What causes this? I think basically it is lack of growth. I think these people are afraid of freedom. Perhaps they were raised this way. Some people are raised in very legalistic homes, and they don't have the confidence of the Lord in their lives. Some people need constant support. They have to be propped up to be assured. They are, in a word, like children.

It's one thing to be *childlike,* but it's quite another to be *childish.* It's a marvelous thing for a little baby to cling to Mother. It's a terrible thing for a 40-year-old man to cling to a set of rules and regulations. Basically it boils down to a lack of spiritual knowledge.

In 1 Corinthians 8 Paul made it very clear that knowledge, love, and conscience go together. As we grow in knowledge and as we practice love, we grow in the Lord and develop a strong conscience.

Hebrews 5:12–14 pretty well summarizes this situation: "For when for the time ye ought to be teachers, ye have need that one teach you again the first principles of the oracles of God, and are become such as have need of milk, and not of solid food. For everyone that useth milk is unskillful in the word of righteousness; for he is a babe. But solid food belongeth to them that are of full age, even those who by reason of use have their senses exercised to discern both good and evil." In other words, when the child of God feeds on the Word of God (the food) and obeys the Lord (the exercise), then he grows. Conscience grows as it is exercised.

How do you hinder conscience from growing? Depend on other people to tell you what to say and do. Have a list of rules and regulations, some external standards (other than biblical standards) that guide you in making your decisions.

We have had the joy of raising four children. When they were little, we had to have rules and regulations. We had to say, "You *don't* go near the highway. You do not leave the back door open—the baby may fall down the stairs. You do not leave a knife on the table—the baby may pick it up and get hurt." But as the children grew older, flexibility moved into our home, and we started operating, not by rules and regulations but by love and principles.

We live by certain principles. We want our children to grow. We want them to be able to exercise discernment. We can't constantly be making their decisions for them. How terrible it would be if God handed us a little rule book that told us what to watch on television, what to read in the newspapers, and what to do here and what to do there. We would never grow. We would never exercise our muscles.

The cause of a weak conscience is lack of knowledge (the window is not letting in the light), lack of exercise, and a fear of freedom. Some ministries keep people weak so that they might be able to manipulate them and make them do what they want them to do. My task as a minister of the gospel is to help you grow, which leads us to our third topic.

The Cure for a Weak Conscience

What is the cure for a weak conscience? I'll tell you what the cure is not. It's not scolding, and it's not beating weak saints over the head!

If your little child is lying in bed saying, "Daddy, there's a bear under my bed," you know very well there's no bear under the bed. But scolding won't solve the problem. What do you do? You go in, you turn the light on, you put your arms around the child, you assure the child that Daddy and Mommy are there. After a while the child laughs and says, "Well, I guess there's no bear under my bed."

The "little children" in our churches with weak consciences need love, truth, and exercise.

Ephesians 4:15 gives us the recipe: "Speaking the truth in love." Love without truth is hypocrisy, but truth without love is brutality. We don't want either extreme. If you have knowledge without love, that's tyranny. If I know something you don't know, I can intimidate you with what I know. But love without knowledge could be anarchy—allowing you to do whatever you want to do. Knowledge and love must be balanced.

In 1 Corinthians 8 Paul made it very clear that we must never deliberately offend a person's conscience. Conscience attaches itself to the highest standard the person knows. We don't *blame* the person for not knowing more; we *help* the person to know more. We open the Word of God and teach him.

Romans 14 and 15 give us three instructions for helping those who have a weak conscience. First, receive them. "Him that is weak in the faith receive ye" (14:1). Don't argue with them, receive them. Don't argue about music, translations, or worldliness, just receive them. And receive them in love! Don't judge one another. Don't condemn one another. Learn to be tolerant of one another. A mature person understands that other people can be different. Being different doesn't mean being worse or being better, it just means being different. So receive them.

Second, edify them. Paul told us very clearly in Romans 14:13–23 to edify them, to build them up, to help them grow.

And third, Romans 15 says we should please them. "We, then, that are strong ought to bear the infirmities of the weak, and not to please ourselves" (v. 1). A little baby is catered to. The baby is pleased (not pampered, not spoiled), and the parents give in to the baby. Why? The baby lacks understanding and needs a time of transition, an opportunity for growth.

Why do we receive the person who has a weak conscience? That we might be able to edify him. Why do we please him? That we might be able to edify him. Why do we share the truth in love? That we might help him grow out of a weak conscience into a strong conscience.

I think the mistake we're making in our churches today is that we receive people who have a weak conscience *and then we keep them that way!* That is unbiblical! We must help them to grow. Romans 14 makes it very clear that our task is to love them, to please them, and to receive them—not so that we can argue with them and judge them but to help them grow so they, in turn, can help other Christians grow.

I think that many of the problems in churches today are caused by people who have a weak conscience. They are critical, they are easily offended, they are unstable, they lack knowledge. It's tragic when these people get into places of leadership because then they make everybody else remain babies.

In the home, the older children help the younger children grow up. When we have in our church a Christian with a weak conscience, it's our job to help that person to grow up. It's a marvelous thing when we have this mixture of strong and weak in our churches because those who have the weak conscience remind those who are stronger not to be arrogant and proud but to be tender, loving, and patient. Those who have a strong conscience are to help those with a weak conscience grow up.

May the Lord help us not to have a weak conscience but to grow in him, to have a strong conscience and to help others grow and be strong in the Lord.

15

A Strong Conscience

We have considered the *weak* conscience, and now we want to think about the *strong* conscience. In Romans 14 and 15 Paul dealt with a conflict among the people in the church—some had weak consciences and some had strong consciences.

Paul began by saying, "Him that is weak in the faith receive ye, but not to doubtful disputations" (Rom. 14:1). This means, "Don't argue about doubtful things."

The Christian life contains some doubtful areas that good and godly people have disagreed on down through the centuries. The specific details may change from age to age, but the basic problems are the same. What can a Christian do? How far can a Christian go?

In the Roman assembly the problem centered on food and the celebration of special days. The weak Christians would eat only vegetables, while the strong Christians ate all foods. The weak Christians commemorated certain days that were very special to them, while the strong Christians realized that every day was a special day with the Lord. Unfortunately, the weak Christians judged the strong Christians, and the strong Christians despised the weak Christians.

In Romans 15:1 Paul said, "We, then, that are strong ought to bear the infirmities of the weak, and not to please ourselves." He was talking about being strong in conscience. He was not talking about physical strength but about the spiritual strength that comes when you have a strong conscience.

So the strong conscience is opposed to the weak conscience. Notice that a person can tell when he has a strong conscience. Paul used the word "we" instead of "they": "We, then, that are strong." If you had asked the Apostle Paul, "Paul, are you a man with a strong conscience?" he would have replied, "Yes." Somebody might say, "Well, aren't you being proud?" No, this is not pride at all. If you *know* you have a strong conscience, there's no reason to hide it. If you have a strong conscience, you have some very important responsibilities.

Characteristics of a Strong Conscience

What are the characteristics of a person who has a strong conscience?

Spiritual Knowledge

To begin with, he is *a person with spiritual knowledge.* He knows the Word of God and what it teaches about various matters in the Christian life.

For instance, various kinds of food were a problem in the Roman assemblies. The strong Christian knows that Jesus declared all foods to be clean. Paul knew that God had made everything good. Peter discovered this same truth on a housetop when he was waiting for his dinner to be prepared (see Acts 10:9–16). He was taught by the Lord that all foods are clean. So the Christian with the strong conscience has spiritual knowledge. He is not living according to superstitions, customs, or the Old Testament Law. He's living by New Testament truth. He understands the truth of the Word.

Discernment

Second, *the person with a strong conscience has discernment.* He has exercised his conscience, his spiritual faculties and senses. He knows what is right and wrong and is therefore able to make the right decisions. He exercises his conscience. He's not afraid to obey the Word of God.

Jesus said in John 7:17, "If any man will do his will, he shall know of the doctrine." Obedience results in spiritual knowledge. The person with a strong conscience is discerning because he exercises his spiritual faculties. He steps out by faith and believes and obeys the Word of God.

Enjoyment of Freedom in Christ

This leads us to a third characteristic: *He enjoys his freedom in Christ.* He knows that in Jesus Christ he has freedom, that all things are his and that God gives to us "richly all things to enjoy" (1 Tim. 6:17). He realizes that God is a gracious and generous God, that every good gift and every perfect gift comes down from God (see James 1:17). Therefore, the Christian with a strong conscience appropriates the truth by faith, and he enjoys his freedom.

If you had visited some of the members in the Roman assemblies, you would have seen a contrast between freedom and bondage. The weaker Christians were in bondage. They were living by Old Testament rules and regulations, and consequently they were not enjoying their freedom in Christ. The mature, strong Christians were enjoying their liberty in the Lord because they had appropriated and practiced Bible truths.

Tolerance of Differences in Others

Not only does the person with a strong conscience have spiritual knowledge and spiritual discernment, not only does he enjoy his freedom in the Lord, but *he is tolerant of the differences in others.* This is an important thing. A person with a strong conscience is not easily offended.

We noted that the person with a weak conscience is easily wounded. If somebody does something he doesn't like, he is deeply grieved and offended by it. This is a sign that he has a weak conscience. When a person has a strong conscience, he realizes that good and godly people disagree on some practices, and he does not get offended.

Some years ago a friend of mine was ministering in Scandinavia. He and his interpreter were walking down the street, and my friend began to whistle. His interpreter said to him, "Who is going to preach tonight?" and my friend said, "Well, I'm going to preach tonight." The interpreter said, "Oh, no, you can't preach tonight. No, you just grieved the Lord by whistling." Many of the Christians in that part of the world did not believe that people should whistle. Christians would never whistle in public.

At a conference some years ago another friend of mine was chatting with a pastor. This pastor came from a part of the country where the use of tobacco was not frowned upon too much. This pastor was complaining to my friend because the young people were down at the beach together, and he said, "I don't think that you should permit that." My friend reached over and pulled a package of cigarettes from the man's pocket and said, "Well, you take care of this, and we'll take care of that!"

What was he saying to him? He was saying, "Brother, there is such a thing as geographical Christianity. In some parts of the world some things are frowned upon that may be approved in other parts of the world."

You may say, "But isn't that rather inconsistent?" No, not at all. The Christian who has a strong conscience realizes that good and godly people can disagree on practice. We aren't talking about *doctrine*. The fundamentals of the faith are true regardless of whether you are in Asia, Africa, Australia, or America. But practices have a way of changing with culture. We're talking about this area of questionable things. The Christian who has a strong conscience is tolerant of differences. He realizes that differences do not necessarily mean that one person is better or worse than the other. You will notice changes as you go from place to place and from culture to culture. The person with a strong conscience is not easily offended. The strong believer doesn't stumble and get hurt. He doesn't sit and nurse his wounds. He doesn't get critical. The Christian with a strong conscience enjoys his freedom and is willing to give that same freedom to others.

Responsibilities of the Strong Christian

But the strong Christian also has some responsibilities. Romans 14 and 15 were written to the strong Christian primarily, and these chapters state our responsibilities if we claim to have a strong Christian conscience.

Receive the Weak

Our first responsibility is to *receive the weak.* "Him that is weak in the faith, receive ye, but not to doubtful disputations [questionable things]" (Rom. 14:1). We are not to keep people out of the church fellowship because they haven't grown up yet. The church is God's nursery for helping babies to grow. We have the responsibility of receiving the Christian who has the weaker conscience.

Do Not Argue

Second, we have the responsibility *not to argue with him.* I would strongly advise you not to argue with people about these areas where you disagree. We can discuss principles, we can discuss biblical doctrine; but in areas of taste and custom, there is simply no way to agree.

Do Not Despise the Weak

Third, those who are strong are *not to despise those who are weak.* Romans 14:3 says, "Let not him that eateth despise him that eateth not; and let not him who eateth not judge him that eateth." In other words, the strong Christian is not to despise the weak Christian, and the weak Christian is not supposed to condemn the strong Christian because he enjoys his freedom.

Do Not Cause the Weak to Stumble

Fourth, and this is very important, the strong Christian is *not to cause the weak Christian to stumble.* Romans 14:13 says, "Let us not, therefore, judge one another any more; but judge this, rather: that no man put a stumbling block or an occasion to fall in his brother's way."

This brings us to what Paul wrote in 1 Corinthians 8, 9, and 10. The problem in Corinth was, If you are invited to a feast at the local temple, should you go? After all, that's an idol's temple, and that meat was offered to an idol. Paul said it may not hurt *you*, but it might hurt your weaker brother. If your brother sees you in that temple, he may be tempted to go against his conscience, and you will cause him to stumble. I can do many things that may not hurt *me*, but they might hurt somebody else.

We are not to cause the weak to stumble. We are not to grieve our weaker brother by our liberty. Romans 14:15 says, "But if thy brother be grieved with thy food, now walkest thou not in love." We should walk to please our weaker brother, not to please ourselves. "Let everyone of us please his neighbor for his good to edification" (15:2).

You may say, "Well, why should I give up my liberty just to please my brother?" Because that's Christian love. Why should you use your freedom to cause somebody else to stumble? We have to be very careful how we handle these matters. We should walk in love.

Make Peace

The stronger Christian has another responsibility: *He should make peace.* "Let us, therefore, follow after the things which make for peace" (Rom. 14:19). Some Christians are forever declaring war! They are constantly looking down on people they feel are inferior to them. Paul said, "Don't do that. Do the things that result in peace. What difference does it make whether you eat meat or don't eat meat? The important thing is that your brother and you get along. An unsaved world is watching. Don't be caught fighting one another."

Not only should we make peace, but we should build up the weaker brother. We should do those things that help to edify others. The reason we receive the weaker brother and seek to please him is that we might help him grow up.

131

You cannot force your faith on somebody else. "Hast thou faith? Have it to thyself before God" (v. 22). You cannot push truth down someone's throat and force them to digest it! We have to speak the truth in love (Eph. 4:15). We must demonstrate patience, love, and kindness if we are to help these people grow.

The important thing is for the stronger Christians not to abuse their freedom. In Romans 15 Paul used the Lord Jesus Christ as our example: "For even Christ pleased not himself" (v. 3). Think of the freedom that Jesus deprived himself of so that he might help others! He was the perfect Son of God who knew all things, and yet he deliberately humbled himself, he deliberately limited himself so that he might be able to minister to us. The result, of course, brought glory to God.

"Wherefore, receive ye one another, as Christ also received us to the glory of God" (v. 7). That settles the matter right there. The weak Christian is not to break fellowship with the stronger Christian over such things as amusements, food, Bible translations, different kinds of music, or methods of teaching. It is so easy for the weaker Christian to feel threatened, to get defensive and to say, "I can't fellowship here any more. These people do too many things that are wrong." He never will grow up if he has that attitude. However, if the strong Christians have an attitude of superiority, there will be trouble in the church.

In 1 Corinthians 8:9 Paul warned, "But take heed lest by any means this liberty of yours become a stumbling block to them that are weak." I have the right to enjoy my freedom, but I also have the freedom to give up my rights. That's a part of my freedom in the Lord. I have the right to enjoy all things that God has created. But if, in using that freedom, I rob you of blessing or I hurt you, then it isn't freedom at all. It has become bondage. Those who are strong in the Lord must be very careful not to look down on those who have not matured. However, those who have not yet grown in the Lord ought to start growing. There ought to be such an atmosphere of love, knowledge, and acceptance in the church that the weakest Christian can receive the Word of God and grow.

I suppose you can summarize it by saying that we belong to each other, we affect each other, and we need each other. The strong Christian needs the weak Christian, and the weak Christian needs the strong Christian. We all need the Lord. If we live to please ourselves and to boast about our knowledge and our freedom, then we will cause division, dissension, and destruction in the church. But if we live to please the Lord Jesus and to please one another, if we show preference to those who are weaker, then we are going to help them grow. At the same time, *we* are going to grow, and there will be a beautiful atmosphere of love in the church. The spiritual babies will grow up and help other babies grow up. God's work will progress, and Jesus Christ will be glorified!

16

An Evil Conscience

*H*ave you ever wondered how it's possible for people to do evil things and not be bothered about them? Some people can lie and never lose any sleep. They can steal and do other evil things, and it never seems to upset them. But you and I are bothered by even a little thing until we come to the Lord and get it straightened out. How can some people do evil things and not be disturbed? The answer may be that they have an evil conscience.

"Let us draw near with a true heart in full assurance of faith, having our hearts sprinkled from an evil conscience, and our bodies washed with pure water" (Heb. 10:22). The writer used Old Testament symbolism to convey a New Testament truth. When the priest was ministering in the tabernacle, he had to wash his hands and his feet at the laver so he would not defile the tabernacle. You and I, when we fellowship with the Lord, must be sure that we are washed clean. "Create in me a clean heart, O God, and renew a right spirit within me" (Ps. 51:10). "Behold, thou desirest truth in the inward parts" (v. 6).

What Is an Evil Conscience?

Let's try to understand this concept of an evil conscience by answering several questions. First of all, *what is an evil conscience?* The simplest explanation I think is simply this: An evil conscience is the opposite of a good conscience. A good conscience is effective—it convicts us when we have done wrong, and it encourages us when we have done right. But an evil conscience encourages the person when he does wrong and bothers him if he does something right!

I think Isaiah 5:20 describes people who have an evil conscience: "Woe unto them that call evil, good, and good, evil; who put darkness for light, and light for darkness; who put bitter for sweet, and sweet for bitter!"

In other words, they brag about the things they ought to be ashamed of. Paul wrote about them in Philippians 3:19: "Whose glory is in their shame, who mind earthly things." The things they ought to be ashamed of, they glory in! When they do something good, it disturbs them. Why? Because they don't want to do good, they want to do evil. When they do something to hurt someone else, it doesn't bother them because their inner light has turned into darkness.

This takes us again to Matthew 6 where the Lord Jesus compared conscience to a window that lets in the light: "The lamp of the body is the eye; if, therefore, thine eye be healthy, thy whole body shall be full of light. But if thine eye be evil, thy whole body shall be full of darkness" (vv. 22–23). Note this important statement: "If, therefore, the light that is in thee be darkness, how great is that darkness!" (v. 23).

135

Conscience is the window that lets in the light. As we sin against the Lord, that window gets dirtier and dirtier. Finally, the light doesn't disappear, *the light turns into darkness!* That which should guide us into truth guides us into error. This is an awesome thing. Jesus did not say that, as we continue to sin, the light disappears. No, He said a far worse fate will overtake us: The light will turn into darkness! That which should be a blessing to us becomes a curse. That which should help us begins to hurt us.

So an evil conscience is one that calls evil, good and good, evil. It puts darkness for light and light for darkness. An evil conscience does not convict us when we have done wrong. We get accustomed to our sins, and our conscience does not bother us.

What Causes an Evil Conscience?

What causes an evil conscience? I think the simple answer to that question is this: *a failure to be serious about sin.* It is dangerous to take sin lightly. If I can, without feeling guilty, do something today that six months ago would have bothered me, then I may be starting to get an evil conscience. When you start to take sin lightly, you are moving in the wrong direction—from light to darkness.

I think one reason why many people today take sin so lightly is that they take God very lightly. When we do not have a holy respect for God, then we have no respect for holiness or for God's judgment of sin.

In 1 John 1, John talked about people who try to cover their sin. He pointed out that they cover sin with their speech. "If we say that we have fellowship with him, and walk in darkness, we lie, and do not the truth" (v. 6). They begin to lie to other people. They say, "Oh, yes, I'm in fellowship with God." They sing the songs and give their testimonies, but they're walking in the darkness.

In 1 John 1:8 we see them start to lie to themselves: "If we say that we have no sin, we deceive ourselves, and the truth is not in us." They can tell the same lie so often that they really start to believe it! First John 1:10 says, "If we say that we have not sinned, we make him a liar, and his word is not in us." Next they lie to God! They might go through a form of prayer, but they aren't really praying. It is all a masquerade.

A good conscience functions properly. But if we sin against that good conscience, we develop a defiled conscience. "Unto the pure all things are pure, but unto them that are defiled and unbelieving is nothing pure; but even their mind and conscience is defiled" (Titus 1:15). A good conscience becomes defiled because the window starts to get dirty. The more we sin against the Lord, the dirtier that window becomes.

This can lead to a *seared* conscience. "Speaking lies in hypocrisy, having their conscience seared with a hot iron" (1 Tim. 4:2). This image is not difficult to understand. When your skin is burned, it develops a calloused area of scar tissue, and that area loses its sensitivity. In a similar manner your conscience can be seared.

First, a good conscience becomes a defiled conscience, and then a defiled conscience becomes a seared conscience. It's possible to get to such a low point in our lives that sin doesn't bother us anymore. We can lie with a straight face, and it doesn't bother us one bit. This, of course, leads to an evil conscience.

What Are the Evidences of an Evil Conscience?

Someone may ask, "How can I know if I have an evil conscience?" Let me give you some evidences of an evil conscience.

Playing with Sin

The first evidence is that *you play with sin*. Whenever you start playing with sin, you don't take it seriously. The person with an evil conscience can play with sin and not be worried.

Shallow Confession and Shallow Repentance

Another evidence is *shallow confession and shallow repentance*. Whenever I make excuses instead of confessing my sin to God, I know something is wrong inside. The person with an evil conscience can make very shallow confessions and very hasty repentance that is not repentance at all—he's just making excuses.

Measuring Sin

I think another evidence of an evil conscience is that *we start to measure sin*. We try to convince ourselves that there are big sins and little sins. In God's sight sin is sin, and the more understanding we have, the more we'll realize that what we thought were small sins are just as bad as the so-called big sins in our lives. Someone may say, "Well, I haven't murdered anybody. That's a big sin. I've not committed adultery. Therefore, I can get away with these smaller sins."

The British Bible teacher, Dr. G. Campbell Morgan, used to talk about "sins in good standing." I fear that in our churches today there are sins in good standing. We would expel a member for fornication or drunkenness or murder, but what about gossip? What about lying? What about pride? The person with an evil conscience measures sin—he classifies some sins as big and some as little.

Concerned about Reputation

A person with an evil conscience is *more concerned about reputation than about character.* If you have an evil conscience, all you are concerned about is that you don't get caught. And even if you do get caught, you can talk your way out of it! People who are more concerned about reputation than about character will do anything privately if they aren't caught or seen publicly. What a dangerous attitude this is because your conscience begins to decay and become evil.

Arguing with the Truth

I think another evidence of an evil conscience is that *we start to argue with the truth.* When you meet a Christian who is supersensitive about some matter, watch out! He may be developing an evil conscience. You can't talk to him about the subject because he's already made up his mind. He can argue with the truth. He can explain away what he's doing. I have even known professing Christians who used the Bible to support their sin.

Who Can Get an Evil Conscience?

We've asked the questions, What is an evil conscience, what causes an evil conscience, and what are the evidences of an evil conscience? Here's another question: *Can this happen to anyone?* Yes, it can happen to you, and it can happen to me.

It happened to King Saul. I think one of the most tragic biographies in the Bible is that of King Saul. He started off with such great blessings—anointed with the Spirit, surrounded by a group of men who wanted to work with him. He faced great opportunity. He had a marvelous friend, Samuel, who prayed for him. But then Saul got impatient, and he began to lie. He was worried about impressing people. He said to Samuel, "Honor me before the people" (see 1 Sam. 15:30). He became envious of David. And he ended up in the darkness of a witches' cave because God had forsaken him (see 28:7–25). Then he went to the battlefield and committed suicide (see 31:1–6).

It all started when Saul lied to his conscience and played around with sin. King Saul went down into darkness because he had an evil conscience. Those who were his best friends, he treated like enemies. Those who were really his enemies, he treated like friends.

But I would remind you that this also happened to David. In 1 Samuel 24 we read that David cut off the skirt of King Saul's robe when the king was asleep. And this bothered David. The Bible says, "David's heart smote him" (v. 5). David's conscience at this point was so tender that this little action upset him. In 1 Samuel 26 he took the spear and the water jug from Saul, but we don't read that his heart smote him when he did it. A few years later David took Bathsheba and murdered her husband, and for a whole year he covered his sin! Was it possible for the sweet singer of Israel to get an evil conscience? Yes! It happened to David and Saul, and it can happen *to you and me!*

Can an Evil Conscience Be Cured?

This brings us to our final question: *Can an evil conscience be cured?* The answer is *yes.* We can come to the Lord and have our hearts cleansed from an evil conscience. First of all, we must confess the sin honestly before God and demonstrate an attitude of true repentance. David, in Psalm 51, gave us a beautiful illustration of how to be broken before God. We need to be cleansed and purged by the blood of the Lord Jesus Christ.

"How much more shall the blood of Christ, who through the eternal Spirit offered himself without spot to God, purge your conscience from dead works to serve the living God?" (Heb. 9:14). We must truly repent of our sin and confess it to God. We must repair any damage we can through restitution or apology. We must be cleansed and purged of our guilt. We must also draw near to God. "Let us draw near . . . in full assurance of faith, having our hearts sprinkled from an evil conscience" (10:22). The author of the Book of Hebrews was talking about cleansing by the blood of the Lord Jesus Christ.

If, in honesty, someone says, "I have an evil conscience," I would warn him: Not only will your light turn into darkness, but you will also cause other people to live in darkness. The tragedy of having an evil conscience is the damage that we do to other people. The husband who has an evil conscience will do damage to his wife and his family. The teenager who has an evil conscience will do damage to his parents and his friends. Think of the damage Saul and David caused.

Is there something in our lives today that we are afraid might be found out? Are we cultivating an evil conscience, being more concerned about reputation than about character? Are we more concerned about what people think we are than about what God knows we really are?

I would issue this warning: If you live with an evil conscience, ultimately it will destroy you. It may not kill you the way it killed King Saul, but it can destroy your joy, your power, your fellowship with God, your character. It will destroy your peace. It will destroy your fellowship with those who love you. But I can say to you on the authority of the Word of God, no matter how dark your conscience may be, if you will come to Jesus Christ and confess your sin in an attitude of true repentance, He will restore you. He will cleanse you. He will wash the window of your soul, and the light will start to shine in again.

Then you will want to be very careful to maintain a sensitive conscience, being obedient to God's will.

May the Lord help each one of us maintain a good conscience, lest we develop a defiled conscience and then an evil conscience!

17

Conscience and Ministry

*C*onscience is important for Christian living. It is also important for Christian service. What Paul wrote to Timothy in 1 Timothy 1:19 must be taken to heart by all of us who serve Jesus Christ: "Holding faith, and a good conscience." It's much easier to hold to the faith and to be evangelical and orthodox in theology than it is to have a good conscience. It is unfortunate that occasionally bad publicity is given to some Christian worker who was true to the faith but who didn't have a good conscience. As a result, he got into trouble.

Conscience is important if we are going to be effective in our ministry. Let's look at five different areas of ministry where conscience is vitally important.

Winning the Lost

First of all, conscience is important in the area of *winning the lost.* After all, that's why we're in the world—to win the lost to Jesus Christ.

Romans 9:1–3 says, "I say the truth in Christ, I lie not, my conscience also bearing me witness in the Holy Spirit, that I have great heaviness and continual sorrow in my heart. For I could wish that I myself were accursed from Christ for my brethren, my kinsmen according to the flesh."

The Apostle Paul had a great burden to reach his own people, the Israelites. Even though Paul was called to be a missionary to the Gentiles, he always had a burden for the Jewish nation. Paul's burden was a *real* burden, not an artificial burden.

I trust that I will not be misunderstood as I say this, but I fear that sometimes soul winning, or witnessing, becomes a fad. Some preachers and teachers make soul winning a "Gospel hobby." They are forever counting how many they witness to or how many they win to Christ. And I think this is wrong. I think it's good to be able to report statistics. Mr. Spurgeon used to say that those who criticize statistics usually have none to report. I see nothing wrong with praising God for people who have been won. But only God knows how many of them are true believers. The important thing is not the report; the important thing is your motivation.

Paul's burden was real, not artificial. He said, "My conscience also bearing me witness" (v. 1). The Holy Spirit witnessed to the fact that Paul had a sincere love for lost souls. We need that same love today.

It's very easy for me as a preacher to preach something from the Bible that I don't really feel in my own heart, and that's dangerous. It's possible for Sunday school teachers to teach a lesson to their students that has no meaning for them at all. It's possible even for us to witness to people simply out of obligation and not because of true concern or love for them.

Peter had something to say about this in 1 Peter 3:15–16: "But sanctify the Lord God in your hearts [sanctify Christ as Lord in your hearts], and be ready always to give an answer to every man that asketh you a reason of the hope that is in you, with meekness and fear, having a good conscience, that, whereas they speak evil of you, as of evildoers, they may be ashamed that falsely accuse your good manner of life in Christ."

We must have a good conscience as we witness. If we don't have a good conscience, we will have no power in our witness. If, while I'm sharing the Gospel with others, I know that in my own heart something is wrong, God cannot bless.

Planning for Service

The second area where we must have a good conscience if we're going to minister effectively is in *making our plans for service*. In 2 Corinthians 1:12 we read, "For our rejoicing is this, the testimony of our conscience, that in simplicity and godly sincerity, not with fleshly wisdom but by the grace of God, we have behaved ourselves in the world, and more abundantly toward you."

Let me give a bit of background here. Paul had promised to come to Corinth and perhaps even spend the winter with them. He was going to take up a collection for the poor Jews in Jerusalem. Paul made his plans and shared them with the Corinthians, and then he had to change his plans. The church accused Paul of being devious and of not meaning what he said. They said, "When Paul says yes, he means no, and when Paul says no, he means yes." Paul spent several chapters in 2 Corinthians straightening out this disagreement and misunderstanding.

I have had to cancel meetings. I have received letters from people who have been upset with me because circumstances forced me to change my plans. I recall that, when my mother had a stroke and I had to change all my plans, a few people where I was to speak in conferences were very unhappy because I had to rearrange my plans.

At times I have said to people, "I'd like very much to come and minister," and then God has changed my plans. The important thing is that you have a good conscience.

We make plans and say, "If the Lord wills, we'll do thus and so." We can't guarantee that this is what God wants us to do. We don't always know every detail about the will of God for our service. The important thing is for us not to scheme and lie but to be open and honest. Paul said, "My conscience testifies to me that I was sincere. I had integrity. I was not using fleshly wisdom. I'm sorry it didn't work out the way you wanted it to work out, but my conscience bears witness that I was not wrong."

Someone has said that faith means living without scheming. If you start scheming in your ministry, watch out! You're not living by faith.

Ministering God's Word

The third area of ministry where conscience is important is *in the ministry of the Word of God*. Second Corinthians 4:2 says, "But [we] have renounced the hidden things of dishonesty, not walking in craftiness, nor handling the Word of God deceitfully, but by manifestation of the truth commending ourselves to every man's conscience in the sight of God."

Second Corinthians 5:11 says, "Knowing, therefore, the terror of the Lord, we persuade men; but we are made manifest unto God, and I trust also are made manifest in your consciences."

Paul was saying two things here: When we minister the Word of God, our conscience is open before God. Our conscience is also open before people. At times when I have heard an individual sharing the Word of God, my conscience has begun to bother me because he was not handling the Word of God accurately. Paul was telling us that, as we share the Word of God, we ought to have a conscience void of offense before God and before people.

Some people deliberately twist the Word of God; they use dishonesty and craftiness. Some have schemes whereby they can prove anything from the Bible. But when you use the Word of God honestly, when you use the Word of God with a clear conscience, then God can bless.

If I am ministering the Word of God and my conscience is open before you and before God, then the Spirit can use the Word and bless your life. But if I'm being deceitful and crafty, if I'm handling the Word of God in some devious way, then it's impossible for God to bless. Unfortunately, many people don't know the difference—they listen to a speaker and do not know whether or not he's using the Word of God accurately. If your conscience is functioning as it should, the Holy Spirit of God will give you discernment.

Not only should we be honest in ministering God's Word, *but we should practice what we preach.* It's easier to preach than it is to practice. In 1 Timothy 3:9–10, Paul wrote to the deacons: "Holding the mystery of the faith in a pure conscience. And let these also first be proved; then let them use the office of a deacon, being found blameless." Proved in what way? Let them prove that they practice what they believe. "Holding the mystery of the faith in a pure conscience." In other words, we should not be orthodox in belief only but also orthodox in behavior. It is important that we have a good conscience as we minister God's Word, not twisting the Word of God, not making the Word of God say something it doesn't say. No preacher or Sunday school teacher should prepare a sermon or a lesson and then try to find a Scripture passage to fit it. Go to the Word of God first and find out what it says. Then prepare the message or the Sunday school lesson.

Facing Criticism

Conscience is important in our ministry, not only in winning the lost, in making our plans for service, and in ministering God's Word but also *in facing criticism.*

First Corinthians 4:1–5 says, "Let a man so account of us, as of the ministers of Christ, and stewards of the mysteries of God. Moreover, it is required in stewards, that a man be found faithful. But with me it is a very small thing that I should be judged of you, or of man's judgment; yea, I judge not mine own self. For I know nothing against myself, yet am I not hereby justified; but he that judgeth me is the Lord. Therefore, judge nothing before the time, until the Lord come, who both will bring to light the hidden things of darkness, and will make manifest the counsels of the hearts; and then shall every man have praise of God."

Paul was severely criticized by the Corinthian church. They compared him with Peter and with Apollos. They said that Paul was a dynamic letter writer but a very boring preacher. They had a lot of criticism against Paul and his ministry. Paul said, in effect, 'The criticism doesn't bother me. Men can criticize me. I don't even criticize myself." The word translated "know" that he used in the phrase "I know nothing against myself" (or "I know nothing by myself") comes from the same root as the Greek word for conscience. He was saying, "My conscience does not accuse me." Then he added, "Yet am I not hereby justified." In other words, it's possible to have a clear conscience and still be wrong. But Paul was saying, "When you face criticism and you know you are right, your conscience gives you strength, and you can take it."

Years ago Dr. A. W. Tozer taught a good lesson. He said, "Never be afraid of honest criticism because it can always help somebody. If the person who criticizes you is wrong, you can help him. If he's right, he can help you." So honest criticism can be helpful. But sometimes in the ministry there's a lot of dishonest and malicious criticism and a lot of complaining. Paul said, in effect, "If your conscience is clear, you can take it because the Lord is with you."

Opposing False Doctrine

A final area where we must use conscience wisely as we minister is *in opposing false doctrine.*

First Timothy 1:18–19 says, "This charge I commit unto thee, son Timothy, according to the prophecies which pointed to thee, that thou by them [the prophecies] mightest war a good warfare, holding faith, and a good conscience, which some, having put away concerning faith, have made shipwreck."

How do you fight the battle against false doctrine? With faith and a good conscience, with the Word of God and a good conscience. We have to be orthodox in our theology, and we also have to be orthodox in our living. Some people think they can battle against the lies of the Devil even though they have a bad conscience. I want you to know that when the Devil finds a defiled conscience, he makes a beachhead there. Satan likes nothing better than to find a Christian worker who's not practicing what he preaches. Satan won't stop him from *preaching* the truth, just as long as he does not *live* the truth. That is what happened to King Saul. He began gradually to move away from the truth of the Word of God, and finally he ended up in ruin and in disgrace.

The Devil can use an orthodox preacher to further his cause by wrecking the preacher's testimony. Nothing can do more damage than a good man who falls into bad living.

Conscience is a mighty weapon for fighting false doctrine and fighting the battles of the Lord.

Recently I have been rereading a biography of Martin Luther, the great reformer, and he said this when he was on trial: "Unless therefore I am convinced by the testimony of Scripture, or by the clearest reasoning—unless I am persuaded by means of the passages I have quoted—and unless they thus render my conscience bound by the Word of God, I cannot and I will not retract, for it is unsafe for a Christian to speak against his conscience. Here I stand, I can do no other; May God help me! Amen!"

How could this man stand against nations and religious leaders and have that kind of courage? He had a good conscience. When your conscience is bound by the Word of God, then you can courageously oppose false doctrine.

We have discussed five areas of ministry where conscience is vitally important. If we are going to win the lost, our conscience must testify that we have a sincere burden for people. We aren't out just to win converts and count numbers. If we are making plans for ministry, our conscience must witness that we are not scheming and trying to promote our own selfish purposes. As we minister God's Word, our conscience must testify that we're not twisting the Word of God or handling it in some deceptive way. As we face criticism (and all of us face it), we must be sure that our conscience is clear. If the critic is right, he can help us. If he's wrong, he can't hurt us. Our conscience bears witness that we're serving the Lord. Finally, as we fight the battles of the Lord and oppose false doctrine, conscience is a mighty weapon to give us victory.

What is the condition of your conscience today? Would it not be good for all of us to go before the Lord and find out from Him if we have a good conscience, a conscience void of offense, a pure conscience? If we have a good conscience, we can minister effectively to the glory of God.

18

Conscience and Government

*A*s Christians our citizenship is in heaven, but we are also citizens of this world. We may be pilgrims and strangers walking through this world, but we still must relate to people around us and to civil government.

The classic chapter in the New Testament on the Christian and government is Romans 13: "Let every soul be subject unto the higher powers. For there is no power but of God; the powers that be are ordained of God" (v. 1). Paul stated here that authority has been established by God. And he went on to say in this chapter that there are four reasons why the Christian ought to obey government: to avoid wrath or punishment (vv. 1–4); for conscience' sake (vv. 5–7); for love's sake because love is the fulfillment of the law (vv. 8–10); and for Jesus' sake because the coming of the Lord is near (vv. 11–14).

I want us to focus on verse 5 where he says we should be subject for conscience' sake. Is it ever right for a Christian, for conscience' sake, to disobey the government? The answer is yes, *but* we must be very careful how we do this. There is such a thing as Christian civil disobedience, but we must be very careful as Christians how we function in this area.

Biblical Examples

Let's begin first of all with some biblical examples of people who did defy the government although they showed respect for the authority.

Jewish Midwives, Moses' Parents

According to Exodus 1, some Jewish midwives were commanded by Pharaoh to kill all the boy babies born to the Jewish mothers. They refused to do it, and as a consequence, they had to answer for that. They practiced civil disobedience. They respected the government even though they disobeyed what they thought was a wrong law. Moses' parents also refused to obey the same law (see Heb. 11:23).

Daniel and His Friends

Daniel, of course, also comes to mind. According to Daniel 1, Daniel refused to eat the food that was put before him. I appreciate the gracious way that Daniel took care of this problem. He did not make a nuisance of himself. He did not try to intimidate the man who was in charge. Rather, he tried as much as possible to live peaceably with all men. He refused to eat the food that had been offered to idols, food that no dedicated Jew could eat. He disobeyed the law even though he showed respect for the government.

In Daniel 6 we read that a law was passed forbidding the people to pray or to make a request of anyone except the king for thirty days. Daniel, of course, broke the law. He had his regular times of prayer, and he was arrested for it and thrown into the lions' den. You'll recall, of course, that God delivered him from the lions' den and honored His name through Daniel. Daniel respected the authority, but he did not obey the law.

The three Hebrew men refused to bow down to Nebuchadnezzar's image, and as a result, they were thrown into the fiery furnace (see Dan. 3). They practiced civil disobedience. They respected the government, but they did not obey what they knew was a wrong law.

Jeremiah

When you read the Book of Jeremiah, you discover that the Prophet Jeremiah regularly was disobedient to the government. For example, he said that the city should surrender to the Babylonians. People called Jeremiah a traitor to the Jewish nation. Imagine, surrendering to the Babylonians! But this was the message God had given him. Jeremiah refused to go along with the politics of his day. He refused to promote the alliances that the unbelieving king was making as he tried to solve his political problem. Jeremiah was considered a traitor. He was arrested and was put in the dungeon, and yet Jeremiah stood true to the Word of God.

Peter and the Other Apostles

I suppose the greatest example in the New Testament is that of Peter and the other apostles. In Acts 4 they were arrested, and they stood before the Sanhedrin to give their testimony. "But Peter and John answered and said unto them, Whether it is right in the sight of God to hearken unto you more than unto God, judge ye. For we cannot but speak the things which we have seen and heard" (vv. 19–20). "Then Peter and the other apostles answered, and said, We ought to obey God rather than men" (5:29). They showed respect for the government, but they did not obey the law.

These are examples from the Bible of people who practiced what is known today as civil disobedience. That title comes from an essay that was written by Henry David Thoreau, the American naturalist. He refused to pay his poll tax because he would not support the Mexican War, and so he spent one night in the Concord, Massachusetts, jail. He inaugurated this thing called "civil disobedience." Gandhi read that essay, and it helped him in his battle for freedom in India. Many of the modern civil rights leaders have followed the principles of Thoreau in practicing civil disobedience.

Principles to Follow

Let's gather some basic principles from these examples for us to follow. Knowing the principles is very important.

Total Control

If you are going to practice civil disobedience, be sure that your conscience controls *all of your life and not just one area.*

I read about university students who refuse to go into the army because of conscience. But their conscience doesn't bother them when they get drunk. Their conscience doesn't bother them when they wreck an automobile at high speed. Their conscience doesn't bother them when they cheat on examinations. I have a hard time believing a person is conscientious about war when he is not conscientious about anything else.

And so the first principle is this: Conscience must control *all of our lives* if we are going to practice civil disobedience. If I see someone who has a good conscience, someone who's walking with God, someone whose conscience guides him day by day, and that person refuses to go to battle, I would accept it. I would believe that he is conscientiously objecting to bearing arms and being honest about it.

It may interest you to know that D. L. Moody, the great evangelist, probably would have been a conscientious objector. He said he simply could not bear arms. Many people, for conscience' sake, will not go to war. They will help in other ways—in the hospital, for example—but they will not bear arms.

If your conscience controls *all of your life* and you're seeking to glorify God, then you can practice civil disobedience.

Biblical Conviction

Second, you must base your disobedience on *biblical conviction*. In other words, you are disobeying human law because you are obeying God's law. The midwives knew that they should not kill. Therefore, they obeyed God, not people. Daniel knew he could not eat food that was prohibited to the Jews. Daniel knew he could not pray to a man instead of to God. The Word of God makes it very clear that idolatry is wrong. The three Hebrew men who were thrown into the furnace knew it was wrong to bow down to an idol. They had definite biblical convictions.

The apostles had been *commanded* to preach, beginning in Jerusalem. They had definite biblical authority behind their convictions.

There are areas in politics and government where good and godly people disagree. Don't make these areas a test of fellowship or spirituality. If you have a biblical conviction about a matter, then that's fine—you hold to it—but don't force your convictions on other people. Good and godly people disagree on some areas. But on the broad areas of life the Word of God is very clear. It's wrong to murder, it's wrong to steal, it's wrong to bow down to idols.

Courtesy

It takes courage to practice civil disobedience, but *be sure you practice courtesy with your courage*. I am impressed with the fact that each of these persons in the Bible who practiced civil disobedience showed courtesy, kindness, and love. They were not burning down buildings. They were not militantly calling people names. In fact, they did just the opposite. They went the extra mile to try to work these matters out in a respectful way. It is possible to respect the authority and still disobey the law. It is possible to be obedient to God and still be disobedient to people.

Daniel could have gotten his guard into trouble. Instead, Daniel said, "Let's try my diet out for ten days. If, at the end of ten days, it doesn't work, we'll work something else out." Daniel had no right to get his guard into trouble. You have no right to get somebody else into trouble because of your convictions. We must respect other people's convictions as well.

I think this is why Paul urged us to pray for those in authority. "I exhort, therefore, that first of all, supplications, prayers, intercessions, and giving of thanks, be made for all men, for kings, and for all that are in authority, that we may lead a quiet and peaceable life in all godliness and honesty" (1 Tim. 2:1–2).

Opportunity for Witnessing

If you're going to practice civil disobedience, *be sure it provides an opportunity to witness*. This is important. We aren't just opposing some bad law, we are seeking to glorify God. Everything we do as Christians affects how people view the Bible. It affects what people think of Christians. It affects their attitude toward the Gospel. I must ask myself, "When I'm all through with this battle, will it be easier to win people to Christ? Will it be easier to witness to them? Will God be glorified?"

Titus 3:1–2 says, "Put them in mind to be subject to principalities and powers, to obey magistrates, to be ready to every good work, to speak evil of no man, to be no brawlers, but gentle, showing all meekness unto all men." That's hard to do, but it's easy to understand. When those who claim to be practicing civil disobedience are brawling and fighting with malice and meanness, I have a hard time believing it comes from a godly conscience. We should look for opportunities to witness.

The Jewish midwives brought glory to God. Daniel was able to bring glory to God. The apostles brought glory to God, and people were saved because of the way they behaved. I fear that some civil disobedience is just plan meanness coming out of people's hearts. They just don't like the government, and so they use conscience as a cover-up for their own maliciousness.

Example of Christ

Follow the example of Christ. First Peter 2:13–25 makes it very clear that Jesus was meek and lowly, that He committed Himself to those who were abusing Him, and that He took it patiently for conscience' sake. Peter wrote: "Submit yourselves to every ordinance of man for the Lord's sake, whether it be to the king, as supreme, or unto governors. . . . For so is the will of God, that with well-doing ye may put to silence the ignorance of foolish men" (vv. 13–15). We're not supposed to have a big mouth and clenched fists—we're supposed to follow the example of Christ.

The Lord Jesus lost *all* of His civil rights. Herod didn't help Him, Pilate didn't help Him, the Jewish priests didn't help Him. Jesus was under three different jurisdictions—Herod, Pilate, and the Sanhedrin. He lost His civil rights, and yet He meekly served and obeyed His Father. We should follow the example of Christ.

Obligations and Peacemaking

Let me share two concluding remarks: First, we are supposed to render to Caesar the things that are Caesar's (Matt. 22:15–22).We have certain obligations. I appreciate police protection and fire protection. I appreciate the streets I drive on. I appreciate city government. I should therefore take my share of the responsibility. We should give to Caesar the things that are Caesar's and to God the things that are God's. And when they conflict, we must serve God first, but let's be sure we're doing it God's way on the basis of his Word.

Second, Romans 12:18 says, "If it be possible, as much as lieth in you, live peaceably with all men." Sometimes it isn't possible, but if it is possible, we must make peace. I think Paul was suggesting in Romans 12:18 that, before you become militant, you try the peaceful solution. That's what Daniel did. That's what the apostles did. If *others* declare war, we can't help that. We ought to obey God rather than people, but let's be careful that as we obey God we also glorify God. When we practice true Christian civil disobedience, God will get the glory.

Warren W. Wiersbe has served as a pastor and teacher and now focuses his energies on writing, teaching, and conference ministry. He lives in Lincoln, Nebraska, and is the author of more than 150 books, including *The Dynamics of Preaching* and *Through the Year with Warren W. Wiersbe.*